DICK: A VERTICAL ELEGY

DICK
A VERTICAL ELEGY

SAM TRUITT

PREFACE
KIMBERLY LYONS

LUNAR CHANDELIER PRESS

© 2014 Sam Truitt

Lunar Chandelier Press
Brooklyn, New York
lunarchandelier@gmail.com

Cover and book design by Julie Harrison, www.julie-harrison.com.
Cover image by permission, derived from *Samuel F. B. Morse*,
computer produced portrait in Morse code symbols (1999), by Ken
Knowlton. www.KnowltonMosaics.com

The author thanks the Fund for Poetry and the Howard
Foundation for their support.

The publisher and author thank the editors of PEN America's PEN
Poetry Series where an excerpt of this work originally appeared.

Library of Congress Cataloging-in-Publication Data

Truitt, Sam
 Dick : a vertical elegy / Sam Truitt ; introduction by Kimberly
Lyons.
     pages cm
  ISBN 978-0-9846076-6-2
1. Kennedy, John F. (John Fitzgerald), 1917-1963--Assassination-
-Poetry.
2. Morse code--Poetry. I. Title.
  PS3620.R85D53 2013
  811'.6--dc23

                            2013031915

Manufactured in the United States of America

For my sisters

PREFACE

There was not enough time to see, her eyes wide open under water. This line might be from a detective story—the dick on a high-speed boat chase suddenly catapulted into the Bay of Naples, or describing a corpse in a swimming pool. But another possibility is that it refers to or at least reminds us, obliquely, of Ophelia. Indeed, this is a line from Sam Truitt's *Dick: A Vertical Elegy* in which Shakespeare's tragedian consciousness is so at work and most acutely in the stitched lines of stage direction that sew the netting of the Morse-coded passages to the cloth of the poem. *To slip past, we must not tear at the meshes,* Truitt offers, helpfully, near the outset.

What could eradicate the memory of Sir John Millais' lushly mesmerizing portrait of Ophelia, her milky eyes staring still into something seen and known hidden there in the forested knoll. *Who's that hiding in the treetops?*

Ophelia haunts. We remain, watching her pass carrying her knowledge in the flowers of her words: *Living with what I know... To actually write—it out—of my head. To focus on a word.* We want to know, desperately, what Ophelia knows and what she took with her into the stream into which she slid—or was pushed.

Or do we? *Dick* reviews with us a plurality of psychological/ ontological/political positions. *History is rife with such master reverse cons.... Wreathed in propaganda and ruled by a scarecrow of warning....* And, *The information we give up—as individuals and as a pack—is consummately harvested to manipulate us.*

Dick haunts also with its knocks *within* and ghosts who enter

and exit; its abrupt arrivals and departures of servants, of res-
cuers—or are they in on the con?—who *enter with drums and
colors* and then are obliterated in the thickets of slashes, dots and
dashes. Alarums are raised and then sink soundlessly into a sea
of churned code.

A recurrent directive in *Dick* is *Be still!*, appropriated from
Maurice Sendak's *Where the Wild Things Are* (published in
1964). Yet it's a phrase from Shakespeare also, used multi-
fariously as order, warning, helpful advisement. It appears in
Brutus's astonishing dying injunction to the man he served—
"Caesar, now be still"—and rings across the waves of writing
that resonate in Truitt's textual positioning, with a Hardy Boys
pack of bumbler's nervous whispering or the sense of a creature
suddenly amidst the doings of monsters. Witty, silly, a relief to
the stealthed, nearly unbearable actions described in other pas-
sages. In another instance in *Dick*, the command to "be still"
is followed by (*Enter E—with the casket*), which realizes yet an-
other, poignant sense: of a squirming child, a three-year-old boy,
perhaps, being told to be still as a casket passes by... *Shaving in
the shower I think of my father—the pain welling up in another
life—and feel it in my throat.*

Lear, *mad, crowned with weeds and flowers*, a dispossessed,
alienated father (just one of the several betrayed and betraying
fathers of Shakespeare to be—lightly—tethered to *Dick*), wan-
ders, deeply, internally processing what he has seen and now
knows, across a landscape wherein (in *King Lear*) a certain Os-
wald ("a serviceable villain" is how Shakespeare dispatches this
character) offers up what *he* knows before being slain. The criss-
crossing of destinies that track across *Dick* is alluded to mostly
in retrospective, brief sightings. *Everybody is running around.
Don't look there!* For all the referencing to cells, there is very
little companionship here, however. None, actually.

Truitt makes meaning portals *with those shards and in a
wilderness of monitors...peepholes* from a variety of sources, in-

cluding the measures of his own political ruminations. Wherever the language comes from or how it arrives, the narrative accumulates in gestures and actions *a scarecrow of* <u>meaning</u> that stutters in the gauze of a text that embeds those motions as a spider web fixates prey. *I stowed white mice in my pockets, edging around the garden with a bow to the wind anchored among the decoys.*

Within *Dick*'s litany of transformations (*I took the form of ivy, the womb of a forest at dawn*) is the sound and sense of the Welsh epic *Ystoria Taliesin*, which demonstrates that a germ, an essence of information, may be transmitted by various transforming beings even in flight. In fact, the riddle of change-ups in appearance is sustained throughout *Dick*. Information comes down, despite *the efforts of carefully self-selected people of strong character able to keep great secrets—and if necessary carry them to their graves.* How hilariously enigmatic that Truitt follows those lines with, from *Hamlet, Enter the* Players *with Recorders*. One of Shakespeare's more mysterious directions—for all the questions of how "recorders" as musical instruments play in the tale—is here punned on as electronic device or human memory ever serving its poetic function: to pass on the story of what happened. And then what happened to what happened.

For all the emphasis on mission asymmetry, however, we retain in general, the idea of theft. That's why we lock on a missing part is one of the elusive shards of writing that might serve as an explanation for one of the impulses behind the composition of *Dick*. From which side of the fence does this phrase originate? Hard to know but one of the 20th century's most asymmetrical missions—the theft of one life—followed perhaps by another, and then another—haunts those of us of a generation. *Enter ghost.* Along with, [*Enter*] Fool [*from the hovel*].

All this and more instigates Lunar Chandelier Press to bring forward Sam Truitt's poetic *thousand-fold echoes*. The matters to which he attends compel us to read and ponder, much like

Gertrude and Polonius viewing the masque devised by Hamlet and his players, and moreover to plunge into the stream of visible and invisible coded text, with our Ophelia (all of them). And then "the unwinding of ciphers," as Truitt has said of this process of reading the code—remains: to ID a conspirator embedded past a few turns in its underlying cryptogram. To wit, here's the first swath of Morse Code deciphered:

O SXZ QXU
POBUCU
HUB XMO
OBMO U
TUFEDELEVOMUDLU
O CBESNO

In the graveyard scene, handed a skull, Hamlet asks: "Whose was it?" But maybe Barnardo already gave away the game when from "a platform before the Castle" he asks: "Who's there?"

Kimberly Lyons
Publisher

DICK

Who's there?
  —Barnardo

Did they do it? At the pump, did Jill hit Jack?

But each place is well and each well a hole encircled by hunters on their hams with spears listening between the broken and whole words into the darkness below for the sound of their breathing and the breathing of the hole in the dark for some fall that is after all cause for image projected staring back into them with red eyes. With hard heavy shoulders. With terror.

"Be still!" --- / ... -..- --.. / --.- -..- ..- / .--. --- -... ..- -.-. ..- / ....- -... / -..- -- --- / --- -... -- --- / ..- / - ..- .-.. . -.. . .-.. . ..- --- -- ..- -.. .-.. ..- / --- / -.-. -.... . ... -. --- But the pigeons are all gone, the dock deserted. There are no voices from here to record the descent.

And the cleaning fluids in the end swirl back into their respective jars.

False statement.

I don't know how I fell asleep last night and don't know if I'm awake now.

True enough.

Summary of scene. Questions. Do we have key sentences? Passages? What results? What does it say about relationship?

This is not enough. And how many holes do I find when I sound "enough"? There is not enough time to come back to see, her eyes wide open under water. .-.. ..- -.... ....- .... --- .-.. / -..- -. .-.. -..- -.- / -- ..- -.. .-.. --- .-.. --- .-.. / .--. --- - --- / ....- -.-. -..- --- -. / -.-. . --- -... --- / -- ..- -.. .-.. --- -.. -.-. -.-. -..- -... ..- --- -.. / - --- -.. / -.- ..- .-.. . -..- --- / --- -.- -..- / ..... -.-. -.. --. --. -.-. -. / ..... -.-. -.. --. --. -.-. -. / -- ..- ... --- -.- -.-. -.- --- -.. / -- --- .-.. ..- --- / .-.. --- -- -.-. --- -.. .-.. ---. / ....- .-.. ..- .... --- -. / -- ..- -. .-. .-.. -.-. -.... -.-. --- -.. / .-.. ..- -...

-.-. -..- --- -.. --. / .-.. .-.-. --- / .-.. . -.-. --- / --- -.- -..- / -- .-- -.. - .. ..- -..
--. --- -... / .-.. --- -.. --. .. .... --- -.. / -.- --- -.. ... --- -.- / -.- --- -.. --- -.- /
- . / -.-. --- .-- --- -. / - . -.. - . -.. --. -- --. . I only know what people said
and sometimes wrote and sometimes didn't say and sometimes
didn't write and only now, vein by vein, leaf on leaf, putting to-
gether an arch through which to pass on. Pass out. Pass groan.

Pass tally sticks of loam. Drool. Slurps. Spurts. Squirts. Tears. Ooze.
Gums.

AKA slug. AKA "shining tragic area." AKA "I have walked
this Earth" and in sepulchral silence of afternoon detention
touched, delicate as a bird in flight, check six, the sphincter. ..- -.-
-..- / -- .. -- -- -.-. -..- --- .-.. / -.- .. .-. .-. --- - --- / .... -..- --- -... --- / .-.- -.. .-..
. .-.- --- / ... --- -- -- --- / -.- .. -- -- -.-.- . .--- -.. / --- -.- -.-.- / -- .. -.. -.. - .. -.. .
--. --- -... / --- .-. . --- / -.-.- --- -.. --. / -.-. --- -.-. ..- / -- .. -.. -.. --- -.. --. . .
.... / - . -.- -.. -.. - -.. ... . -.-.- --- -.. / - .. -.. -.. --. -.- --- -.. / -.- --- -.-. .-. --- -.. --- /
. -.. . . .-.-.- / [Bound, passing on the stage to the place of execution,
and B — going before, pleading.] .--. ..- --- -.-. ..- / .... .. -.-. .. ..- -.. --.
--- -. / -.-. -.. -.-. - --- -.- / -.-.- --- -.. / .... ..- --- -.- -.-. -.-. --- -. / -.- -.-.- -.. ..- -.. --.
/ -.- .. -.-. --- -.- .-. ... --- -.-. -.. --- -.. / .... --- -.- -.-. --- / ..- --- .-. -.-. --- -.. --. -.-. --- -..
/ -- -.- / -.-. -.- -.- -.- --- -.- -.-. ..- --- -. / .-. -.- .. -.- -.- -.. -.- --- -.. -.- / -.... --- -.. --- /
-- -..- / -.-.- --- -.. -.. . "In the United States there are more spaces
where nobody is than where anybody is," she writes.

A few trees stick out, MRX.

We all came here for the cleavage and left embarrassed.

GIGO.

Charlie Mike. .--. --- .... -.- -.-.- / -- . -.. / -. .. -.- . --- / -. . --- .-- --
-. .. -.- -.- -.- .-.- / .--. . .-. -.- .- -.. ... --- -.- / -. . --- .-.-.- / ..- -.- . - --- / -....
.... .--. --- .... . -.- --- -.-.- / ..- . -.. .-. -.-.- / - --- -... ..-.- / [Enter a Solider
in the woods. (A rude tomb seen.)] - -..- ... .- -.- .... / -.. . .--- --- / -- ..-
.--- .-. ..- --- / .... . / -.- --- .-.. -.- . / .... .-. .. . -.-.- --- .-. . / .... -.-. --- -.. / .-.. . ..- --.
-. -.- -.-.- / ..- . / -.- -.- .-.-. .-.- -. --- / .-- -.- -.- --- -.-. -.-. . . .--- --- / - .-.- -..
.-.- / -. ..- -.- -- -. -.- .. ..- -.- -.- He or she's either a good criminal or a
bad one, and we have places for both. -- -..- -.- . - .. -.. / -.... --- .-. . .
-.. .. ..- / --. -.... --- --- . .-. .. -.- -. .- / --- -- . / .... .-.- -.- -.- --- .-. .-. ... - . .-. .-.. -.. ..- .-..

/ ..- -... / ...- --- -... / ..-. ..- ... .- .... / .... . -- The black dog, its face in sections on the mother board waiting to be pawed. Sung to sleep. But never all. At once.

It must be latticed—x's to mark each spot—so that thought's got something to grow on. To latch on. Catch. Gnaw. To claw.

To slip past we must not tear at the meshes the "en" in the above like "net" and "let" and FAHQT. -.-. --- -... ..- .- -... -... --- -..
..- --- .... / -... --- -.-. ..- -... .-. / -.- ..- -... -... ..- .- -.-. / ... --- -- --- .... / -.-.
--- -.. -. ..- -.-. ..- -... / ..- .... .-. ..- / -.-- / -. .-.. / -. --- ... - ..- -- --- -.. /
--.- -..- ..- / .-- --- -... -... ..- -.. / -.. --- --- / .... ..- / .-- .-. -.-. --- -... ..-. .-. --- .-.-.
.- / [Exeunt omnes.] -- --- .... / .... ..- / .... ..- -... / .... --- .-. .--- / - ..- /
-... --- -- --- / ..- --.- -.-. . .-. --- .-. ..- ..- --- .... / ..- / .-. --- -- --- -... / -..
--- .... --- .... / -. --- -- ..- -... / -.- -. --- -... ..- / ..- -.. ..- .- ... -. ..- -.-.
. .- --- .... / .-. ..- ... --- / -.- --- -... .-. --- .... / -- --- -... - / --- --- .... /
-.. .-. --- .... --- .... / .... --- -.. .-. .- --- .... / ..- .- -... -. .-. .- .... / .-. -. --- -..
--- / --- / -- --- -.. ---- -. --- --- / - --- / . -.. .... --- ... .- ... ..- / -.. -.-. -... -.-
.-.. --- .... / -. -.. ..- .- -.. -. --- / -- --- - / .-. ..- .- -... ..- -.-. -.. --- / ..- -... -.-.
--- --- / -..- -.-. ..- ..- / ..- -... .. ..- / .-. --- -. ..- -. .-.-. .- ..- / ..- / - .- .-. --- / .... ..- ..- /
..- --- .... .-. ... . --- -... - / ..-. --- ... .. --- / ..- -- / .- -. . .. --- - ..- / .--- / -..
--- .... --- --- / . .--- --- .... ..- ..- / ..- / -.. --- ... --- --- --- / .--- ..- ... .- -...
.... / -.. --- --- / .-. -. --- .... --- / ..- .... --- ... .-. --- ... -.. -. -... / -- --- ... / -. .
-.. .- .- -... / .... -. -.- / .-. -.- -. .- / -.. --- --- --- / -- ..- / . -- .-. -. --- -... .-. .- --- /
..- / .-. -. --- -- ..- / --- / -.. ..- --- / .-. . --- -... / - --- .... / -. -.- .- .-. --- .-. ..- ....
..- .... / .-. -. --- -... -.. -.- .- ..- / .... -.- --- ... .-. --- .... / .-. .-. --- .-. .-. ... / -.. ..- --- --- /
.... . .-. .--- --- / ..- -.. -.- -. -.-. ..- -.- --- -.-. ..- / ..- - --- -.. .-. ..- / .-. . ... .- -- / -..- .-. --- --- -...
--- .-. --- -.. .- .-. --- .... / .-. -.-. --- -.-. --- / -.... ..- .... .-. ... --- -... ..- - ..- .... / .-. ... --- -... -...
--- / -- . -- / -.. ---- --- Then every day seemed to end with its ass in the air—a red door.

Who's that hiding, in the treetops?

Predictably we referred to it as enargeia because it's destined from the sun who thunders with his spear plucking feathers off a flower.

A little yellow bird. On the window sill.

That's why we can't take things (properties) whole: There'd

be nothing (improperty) left to hold. That's why we can't take too long.

Or when we do facts explode. Faces.

PFM.

Or what we are ignites what we are—metal wings on a stump flung into ECP. To lose, sucking rubber, our faces.

Or Whiskey Delta we are on the back of a monitor, our collaborator. It's a sphere face in. A black sun sucking Alpha. .-. --- ... -- / .-... .-.. ..- / ..... / .... --- / .... -..- .-. --- -... .-.. ..- / --. -... ..- .... ..- ....- ..- / - ..- / ... -- --- -... .... .-.. .-- / - ..- / -... --- .-.- .-.. -. .. ..- --- -.. / ... .- .-. .. ..- / - ..- / - .-.- -... .-. ..- -... ..- / .-. .. .- -. .-. .-.. -.-. / .... / ... -.-. . / ... . .-.. ..- --- --.. / .-. -. -.-. . The sides of the leaves near his brow were whitened, signifying the radiant heat he gave off. --. -.- ... - .-.-. / - -.- / .- --- -- / .- .-. .-. .- -... / --. -.- ... - / . / .... .-. --- ... .- -... .-.- / - -.- / -. --- -... / --- -... .-. .- . -. .-.. / .-. --- -... / -- . --. .-.- / - ..- -... Sure I caught the rhyme but have a jammed a man inside? ---.. .-.-.- / [*Enter* D— *and* C— *with* L—, *ravished;* *her hands cut off, and her tongue cut out.*] -- ---- ..- -... / -.- .-.. --- - .- -... / -.-- -... / .- .-. --- ..- ... / .- .- . / .-. -.-.. / .-. -... ..- -- / --. -... -.. / ... .- .-.-.- - - ..- -... .-.. / -.- / .-. -.-. --- -.- .-.. .-. . .... .-.- / *Knocking without.* - --- .... / --- / ... ..- -- .-.. -.... -.. ..- .... --- / .-. --- - --- / -. --- -- ..- / --- / .-. .- --- -... .-.-. / .-. .- --- .-.. .-.. / .-. .-.- --- .-. ..- .... / -..- -.. . .-... .-. --- / . / .... --- ... --- / -.. --- / --- .-. ....-.. --- -.. .-.. / --- ... ..- --- .-.-.- / *Flourish.* -..- -.. / --- -... ..- .- . .-.- / - ..- / -.-- / - --- -... .... ..- .. --. -.. .-.- / .... / .-. --- / .-. --- .-. ... --. .- -.. . --- .-.-.- / [*Knocking within.*] .... / .-. -.. -.- / ..- -.. .... / .- ..- / -.- .-.. / --- -. ..- / ...- . ... --- -.. .... / .... . -. ..- ..- / -.. --- / .-. -... -.... --- .-. / [*Enter an* Old *Courtier.*] ..... / .-.. .... .-. --- .... / - . .... .-.. -.-. --- .... --- - --- / --- / -.. --- / -.... ..- .... . - . ... / .-. .- -.. .- .-.. / -.-- -.. / -.... -.. / ...- .... --- / .-.- .. -.. --- / -. -.. --- / .-.-.- [*He throws a stone at him.*] .-. ..- -... / .-. --- -.. .. .-. / -. . / -. --- / .-. --- -... .-. .-.-. We wear iron masks. ..... --- ... --- .-.. / -.-. -... --- .-.- .-.- / -.. -- -... .-. .- .- .- / -. --- -.. .-. .-.- -... ... -.. .... ..- .- .-. -... ..- / -.-. -... --- .-.- / -.. -.... -.-.. -.. -.. / ..- -.. - -.. -... -.-. / Got to move like a diamond. Nothing can touch the now. -.-.

-..- -.-- -..- -.- / .-.. -..- -- / -.-. .-- -.. . -- / -.- --- -.. / --. ..- -.. ..- -... --- ...
/ - -.,-- -.. --- -- . .-. .... One day the rebel is sheep for rent or gored.
/ -.- --- ...- --. --- / . .-. . -.. / -.- -.- ... -.- -.-. ..- / . --.. .... ..- - . -- / .-..
-..- -- / .... --- --. -.- -.- / --. ..- .-. ..- ... ..- -... / . .-. . -.. .-.-. / .... . -- - . /
--. --- -... - -.- -. -.. -.- -.. -.- ... / -.-. -.- / --- ...- ..- / --. --- --.. -.-- --- ....
... --- -... .-.-. / ...- ..- / . .-. . -.. / -.-. ..- -... . -- / [*Singing within. Exit*
Ghost.] -.-- --- -... --- -.-. ... --- -... / -.-- --- ....- / -.-. ..- -... ..- .... ..- -.-
... ..- -.-. ... --- -... ..- -.. / - --- ... - -.-. -... -.-. ... -- --- ....- .-.-. / -.-. ..- /
--- .-. ..- -... --- .-. --- -.- / -.- . -.- . -.. / -. -... --- ... - ..- / -.-. ..- -... . -- / -- --- -.
-.- -..- -- / --- --. ... -..- / . .-. . -.. Cloaked in myth and dysfunction
the city bloated lies dreaming before us, but across the desert
(a mirror) at angels 36 the important versus the merely simply
relevant feelings form a convex-concave curve looking up at the
world looking down within an awareness of scale as well as <u>the</u>
scales of the rainbow-hued dragon that rules our CHT.

The small wholesome towns of the republic. Their three
streetlights. The way the roads get weird around the court-
house. The music coming up on the brown-skinned actress and
the doctor with the eyeglasses.

Two day lilies to starboard eating lotus nuts—the sullen man
and the woman who has brought her own earbuds, to gaze into
the spray enraptured.

She could be down there looking up over the rainbow,
stopped at a train crossing singing "Hail to the Meat." ..- .... .-..
--- / .-.. ... --- -... --- / --.- -.- ..- / --- / ....-.. ..- -- --- / ..- .... .-.. --- /
-... --- .-.. --- / .... ..- -.. / -... ..- -....- .-. --- -... --- The penultimate
shot, a dime-sized tunnel through the throat, still smokes.

Today we squeeze FIDO through that hole to reach America.
...- -.-. ..- ... --- / .-.. --- -.. / -... --- .-.. . - --- .-.-. / [*Enter* First Mur-
therer *to the door.*] - ..- / ... --- / .-. --- / .-. . --- ... --- -.-. -... --- / .-. -... . .
.- --- / - --- -... . - ..- / ..- .... .-. ..- --- / .-. ..- -.- / -- --- -... . - --- .-.-. / .... .
/ .-. ..- ..- - --- / -. --- .-. ..- ..- -... / --.- -.- ..- / -- . / .... ..- .-. ..- -... --- /
- ..- / .-.. --- - --- / ... --- / -... . --.- -.- ..- ..- --... --- / - ..- .... .-.. .-.. ..- -... .-..
--- -... / -- ..- .-.-. / [*Enter the* Banditti. *Flourish. Pennants.*] .... .

/ .... ..- / - ..- .... -....- .-.. . .- -... .-.. .--- / .-.. .- .... .-.. .- .-.. .--- / ..- .-. ... .-. -... ..- .-.. .--- / -- ..- / .-. .--- -... ..- .-. ..- / .--- --- -... ..- .-.. .--- / .-. .--- -... --- / --.- -.-. ..- / .--- --- / .... -..- ..- -.. .--- / ..- -... / ..- ... / .... -... ..- -.. .--- / ..- .-.. ..- -... -.. .--- .-.-.- / ..- ... -.. --- -.... .--- / - ..- / - -... .... ..- .- / - ..- / --- -... . ..- -.. / -. .--- -.-. ... .--- / .... -... --- ..- ..- / .... --- -.-. -.. .-. . .-.. .--- / ... .--- / .-. --- .-. .--- / -- --- -.. .-. .--- .... / - ..- .... --- .-. .--- -.. .-. .-. ... .-. .--- / -. --- ..- / .-. --- - - --- / .-. --- -.. / .-. --- .- -.. --- -.. / ..- / -. .-.-.- -.. -.-. / .-. -.- .-.- / .-. .-. -.. / - ..- .... -.. .- -.. .--- / - ..- / .... -.. .-. / - --- .... / -... --- --- -.. / - ..- / ... --- .... .-.-.- / [Knocking within.]
...- --- -- ..- .- .-.. ....-.-.- / [Exeunt omnes with torches] .-. .-..- -.-. .. .- -... .-. .--- / .-. --- -.. / --.- --- -.-. -.-. .--- .... / --. -.... --- .... .-. -... --- --- / .-.- -.-. .-. .-. .-. .--- .-.-.- / [Midday. (Banquet.) Enter Ghost.] - . ..- / .... --- -.. -.-. .- ..- / ..... .-. -.. / ..- . .-.. .-.. / - .-. ..- -.-. .-. .-.-.- / -..- -.. - / -- . .-. .. / .... .-. ..- . .-. -.. / .-. -.. .... --- --- .... ..- .-. / -.-. -.. .- ... ..- / - -.-. --- -.. .-. ..... / - --- .-.. -.. / .-. .-. .-. .. . . / -.. / -- ..- .. .-. ... .-. .-. / - .-. .-. -.. / -- --- .-. ..- . / .... .-. .-. / .-. .-. .. . / - .-. ..- -.. .... / -- --- .-. -.. / ... .-.- .- -... .-.-.- .-.-.- / [Throws up another skull.] .-.- -.. - / . .-.- .-.. / - .-.. .-. --- .... .-. ..- .. / .-. .- .- -.-. ..- .-. -.. / ....- / -..- ..- . .-.. .-.. / .-- ..- --- .-. / - ..- .- .-.-.- / .... -.-. .-. .-. .-.. / - .-.. . .-. .-.. / -.-. . .-. .--. / - .-. ..- .... / ..... --- -.. .... -.. .-. .-.- / - .-. .- .... .-. .-.-.- / .-. .-.. .-.. .-. .-. .. / - ..- -.. / -- .-. .. . / .... . --- --- / .--- -.. .-. / - .- .- ....- / - ..- -.. / -- --- -.. .- / .-.- .-. / ....
--- ... .--. .-. . --. . ..- -.. / .-.. . .-.. . .... .- --. -.. / "Sphincter" equals "riddler" equals "what empties," AKA what makes holes in the hollow in the side of the face in which wasps build Salvo pits. - . ..- / ..- -... - ..- / . .... .-.. / ..- . .-.. / - . ..- .-. .-.-.- / [Enter fighting. Alarums.] - --- .... / .-. .- . .. .- .... / -.-. -.. .. - / -.... --- .... -.. / ..- . --- .-. .. / .-. .- .-.. / .- .. - / .-. .-- --- -.-. .- . --- . .-. / .. -.. .-. .-.. .-. --- . .-.-.- / -... ... .-. .-. / -.- . --- . .-.. .- ....-. -.. .. . .-. .-.- / [Enter O— [with a light] and D—, in her bed (asleep)] .--- .-. -.. - - .- .... / - .-. .-.-.- --. / . .... .-.- / . .- / ..- .- .. . / - .-. .- .-. .... .-. .- .. / - .-. .- / - -. . .-. .. ..- . .-. --.. .. / . .-. . .-.. ..- .-. / - .-. . . / -.- .- .. -.. .- .-. . .-.. .-. . / . .-. .-. / . .- .- - -.. / -.- .- .-.. --- --- .-. . .- .-. .-. / - -- .- .... - .-. .- .-. .- / - .- .. . . .-. .-. .... .- . / -.-. -.. . .-. -.. .- . / -- ..- . .-. .- . .-. ..- . .-. .. / -.- .-. ... .- . .. .- -.. / - -. -.. . .-. ..- . .- .- .. .. . / ..- -.-. .-. -.. ..- - - Send in the jackals. .... . .- -.-. -.. ..- / .-. -- .-. -. ..- -... .-. / -.. .. . .-. .-. .-.
.-.. .-.-.- / [Enter M— (with M—'s head)] .-- .. .-- . / -.... --- -.-. / --..

-..- ..- . -.. --- -.. - ..- -... / ..- .... If man is dust, those who walk the plains are dusty. .--- --- .-.. -..- -. / --- .-.. --- / ... -..- -.-. --- -.. --. / -. --- ... -..- .... / -.-- --- -.. --. /..... . --- .-. --- / . -.. . But why start a fire when everything is?

Except I can't see it. Unless I close my eyes. ..- -.. / - ..- ..- ..- / .-. --- -.. -. -... .-.. ..- .... / --- -.. -.. ..- .. .... / . .... / --- ... ... --- . .-.. / - ..- ...- ..- -.. . -.. / -.- -.. / -- . ... --- -.. --- . -... ..- Three newly born mosquitoes circle his last breath, and his back become the arc of a locust tree bough off which the swing's hung.

Complete, we orbit what is stung.

It will be rain tonight.

Pull chocks. --- -.-. .... . .-.. / --- .-.. .-.. -. --- -... / ..- ....- -- / .-. --- -.. .-.. .-.. -- ..- .... . --- -- / .-.. ..- .-.-. / [*Enter* K— (*disguised as* C—)] .... ..- - / .-. -.-. . -.-. .... / . -.. / --. ... --- -... . --- / -- ..- --- / .... -..- .... .-. .-. . .. ..- .-.. / --- -.. -..- - ..- --- / .-.. . -.-. .... / -- --- -... .-.. --- / .-. -.. -.. --- -.. .-.. .-. .. . .-. . --- Like a vast statue, motionless, inert—except an enormous glaucous, panopticonic eye unblinking guides in total awareness the birth state. --- ... --.. --- / ... --- / .... -.-. --- -... .-. --- / -..- --- .... --- / . .-. / .-.- -.. / ..-. ... --- -... Forces gather that don't have anything to do with it. Or all the arrows seem to hit rump-fed Salvo—not what is needed, wanted.

Or even there.

Nor is most anything (any meeting) distinct, though hope remains that at any point some MOAB may swing and from the side catch the roof and lay bear those people. Having drinks with friends. Beside the pool. Under the candy-striped awning in early evening discussing dick.

Or it's easy enough for a spider to get centered but it's got eight, not seven, legs and only after locking on the ECP in the first place—only then getting hold the rhyme "a car bullets down the hardball."

To look there, after it.

In the shiver drifts a man or two.

Get the sand out of your Charlie and mush. .... --- .... --- -- .--.

--- / -- --- -.- --- .-.. --- -... -..- -.. --. --- -.. --. / --.- -.- .-.. .. -.. / -- .-. .-. ... --- -.-- .-.-.- / [*Lightning. Bodies brought out.*] ... --- -... - .... / ....
--- -- --- -. --- -.. / --- -.. .-. / . .-.-.- --- -... --. / -- --- -... --- -.. --. --- ... / -..
--- / ..- -- .-. .. .- -... --- - --- -... / --- .-. / --- -.. --. / .-.- --- -.. .-.- --- -.. --.
/ .-.- --- . .-. .. .-. / -.. --- -.- -.- --- / . .-. .. .-. .- --- --- ... --- / -... / --- -..
--. / ... --- -.. -. .-.. . .-.. / .-. --- --- .-.. --- / .... --- / .-. -.... . -.. .-. -.. / -- .-. -..
--- -- --- -... --- --- / -.- --- -.. .-. --- -.... . -.. .-. --- -.. --. . --. --. --.-. I prepared a convincing gag,
knowing at our next meeting I could count on trained eyes to
detect any skidmarks, any VDM.

I was away, traveling, balls to the wall OM, broke dick, LLMF,
goldbricked and chopped up, passing from town to town meet-
ing bumf swag. I was OBE and lost track of time.

I've lost touch with many friends, too, and learned we live
seven years here, seven years there and in afterthought, or burn,
another seven years again and we've a life, a glowing structure,
which now I hold pert. - -- . .-.. --- -.. / .... . -- --- -... . .-.. ..- / --- -..- /
.-. --- / .-- --- -.. .-- -- / -.- -.. .. .- -.- .- .... .-. .-.- / -- .- -.. / ..- -.- .... .-..
-... ..- -- . .-. .. ..- / - .. --- -.. / - .. / -.- .--- -.- .-. .- .-.- / [*Enter a* Porter.
Knocking within.].... ..- / --- -..- / .-.. ..- / -.. --- -.. / --- -... / --- -..- /
--- -.- / --- . ..- / --- -.- / .-.- --- / .-.- --- / .-. .--- .--. ..- / .-. .--- -.- / ---
-..- / -.- . -... .-. -.- --- -- .. . .-.. ..- / .-. .-- -- --- .--. ..-.- / [*Flourish.*] -.. --- -..
/ --- -..- / .-. --- -.- .--. .-. -. --- -.. / --- -..- / .-. --- / -.- --- -.. .-. -. .. .- -.-. .-.-.- /
[*Knocking (within).*] -- ..- -.. / --. ..- -.. .-. -.. .-.. -.. / --- -.. .-.. . .--. -.. .- /
-- ..- .-.- .-.. -.... . --.. ..- / .-. --- --- -..- / -.- --- -.. .-. .-.. -.... / --- -.. I stowed the
white mice in my pockets, edging around the garden with a bow
to the wind anchored among the decoys.

He's bigger and grander than anything they offer me.

"How do we know that?" .-.. ..- -.... . -- --- / -.- --- .... . -. .-.-.- /
[*Read aloud.*] -.- ..- - -..- - -..- -.- -.- --- -.. / . .-.. . / .... --- -.-- --- / -.-. -..-
--- .-. .-.-.- / --- -.. . -- / -- ..- -.. .- . .-. .-. .-.. --- / --- -.. . --- -.. / .-.. ..- -...
.-.. -.- --- / . --- -.... . / -.- --- . .... --- -... / --- -.. . --- -.. / .-. .-.- -.- -. --- -.. /
-.-. ..- -.. -.. ..- .-.. / -.- --- -.. -.. .-.-. I don't know dick about poli-
tics and have no grand idea to drag onto the dance floor—but
something must be done to stop those people. - . / --- .... . / -.... ..-

-- -..- .. -.. -.. --- / .... ..- / --.- -..- ..- -.... ..- .... .-.-.- / [*They rise.*] ...- --- ...
-.- --- -- -- ..- -.. / -.-. -... --- -.... .... --- -.. / ..-. -... --- -.. / ..-. -... --- -- --.
--- -.. --. .... -.... .-.- --- / -.- -... ..- .--. .-.-.- / [*Enter, with Drum and Col-*
ors, E—, R—, Gentleman, *and* Soldiers. *Knocking within. Soft*
music.] - -..- / .... --- -- / --- ...- ..- -.... ... ..- ...- ..- -... / --- .-. -. / - -..- /
.... --- -- / .... --- ...- ..- -... / . / -.-. ..- -... --- -- -- ..- ... .- The next
morning I took the polygraph. Electrodes fastened to head and
chest, I went through the prelim pump and dump—the "con-
trol" questions, the "stim" test. I watched the chain-smoking
professor's frail wrists man the knobs—like a corn-holed boy,
his lips frozen in a grimace.

I didn't sweat it. I rolled the pebble between my toes and lied
about everything except the centerfold. Like the prince in the
castle of nine virgins "Rip! rip! rip!" I watched the stylus five
knots to nowhere leap across the cylinder.

I was a volcano vomiting fire.

I was a patent of sagaciousness on the brevity and randomness
of what lives. ..-.- --- .-.... / ... --- -... - .... / - .-.. / ..-. --- -... -- --- --. ..- -..
-. ..- .-.. / --- -... / .... .-.- --- -.- -.. --- / .- / --- ... ... --- .-.-.- / --- .-. .-. /
. / .-.. .-.- --- --- -.. ..... .-.. / . / - .-.. ..- -.. / .... --- -... - / - .-.. --- --. . / - .-.. .-..
/ ....- --- --- -... - .-.-.- / [*Exeunt omnes.* (*Sings*)] -- ..- -.. / .... --- -.- .-.
--- -... ..- / .-.. -... . .-..- -- ..- / --- -... / - ..- -.. -.. . --- / -.-. ..- -.. -.... --- ...-
-.... .-.. -.. . / .-.-. --- -- .-. ..- --- / -. --- .-.. .-. .-. --- - .. .... / .-. --- / - ..- -.. /
.... --- -- / -. --- -... / .-.. .. .. / As for life, we have computers for
that. ... -.-. .-. -.- --- -.. / --- ..- / .-.. --- -. -.. / -- .-. .-. ... --- -.- / --- .-.
-. / ...- --- -.... .... / .-. -.. -.- . -.. .-. .- -... / --- ..- .- -.. / .-. -. --- -.... ....
..- -.. / . / . / -.-. --- .-. .-. .-. ..- -.. / --- ..- / --- -... --- -.. / --- ..- / - --- ...-
. - / -.-. -.. -. -.-. .- ..- / ..-. --- ... -.- ..- .-.. / . / . / -.... --- -- But then again
whenever CenComm barks "all 'something' is 'something'" we
know a problem's en route UYA.

Or absolutes are fudge sticks and always some first most ac-
rimonious son escapes to revenge in cadence state—drag an old
REMF goat by its horns down the mountain and from tree to
tree, stump to stump, blaze in blood a fresh trail down the chain

of command from which there's no turning back, stiff and un-comfortable after long hours rigid with concentration.

The night was gone, and the sun, or "hamburger" as it is sometimes called, rose.

But absent access to primary sources beyond the fence line it's just a story. The little bastard up the hill.

But at least they take a side. All we do's take pictures dedicated to excellent design—the progression of a person from "normal" to tragically extraordinary to whom we've left a makeshift altar of empty ammunition casings entitled "Military Delinquency."

.-. --- -.. .... -.-- -- .-. .-.. . ..- .... / --.. --- .- . ..- -.. / . -.. / -. .--- ... .- /
-.-. --- .-. .-. ..- .- -.. / .... --- -.. / - ..- / -- ..- -.. .... / ..... .-. .. --- -.- . -.. --. /
-. -.- -.. / ..... .-. -. .- -.. -.- .-.. ..- / ..... .-. -. .. .- .. -.. -.-. .. -.. ..- -.. / ..- -.. /
-- --- -... / "Can I get a Pepsi in a red glass?" -. ..- .-.. / --- .- -.. ..... .-.-.
--- -... ..- -.. / ...- --- -.. / - ..- / -- --- -.. -.. ..- -.. ..-.- / [*Storm still.*] -.-
-... --- .- .- / - ..- / ..... .-.. ..- -- / ...- --- -.. / - ..- / --- . ...- --- .-.. .- .-..
--.-..- / - --- .-.. / -. . .--- / -- . ...-. -. .. .- -.. / -.. --- --- . .-.. / -- ..- ..
-... / ...- --- ... .- / .-. .. .-.. .- ..- ... / -.-. ..- -... --- ..- .-. .- ..- -.. ..-.- /
[*Opens a gate. Night. An open place. With* Attendants *meeting a bleeding* Sergeant.] ..- ... .- ..- -.. .. .- . .-.. / ..... .- .. -. .- ... / --. ..- .- ... ..- . - /
--.. . .--- -.. / --.- -.-..- . ...- .-.. ..... .-..- / [L—, *mad, crowned with weeds and flowers.*] -. --- --- -.. / - ..- / ..-. ... ... --- --- ..- -.. / - --- -.-.- / ..
.-. -. .- ..- ... . .-.. / .-.. ..- --. .- -.. / - ..- / --- .-- .-- --- ... .-. .. .-.. .- . ..- / ...- --- -.
/ ...- ... .- ..- ..... / ..- -.. / -... .. . ..- / --. .. ..- ... --- --- .-. .-.. / - --- -.. ..- / -. . .
.--- ---.. / -.. -... --- .-..-. / -.-.. .- -.. .- ... .- .. ..- / -- --- .. .-.. / - ..- / -. ..- .- -.-. ....-. /
.-- ..- .. ..-. / -- ..- . .-.. / -. .-.. .. .-.. / .-.. .... --- -.. / -. ..- . .- / ..- ... ..-.. / - ..- /
-.-. -.. -... .- --- ..-. / .-- ..- -. .. / ...- --- ... ..- / -. ..- .- -.-.- / .-.. ..- ..- .-.. .-.. / --- ...
.... ..- ..... .--.- / [*Enter a* Herald (*pointing at* G—).] -..- ..- / --- .-. .-..
. ...- . .-. .-. ..- . .-.. / ..- .--.. / - .-. --- --. / .... ..- .-- ... . --- .-. .-.. / ..- -.. / .-..
..- / --- .-. -... ..- .- .... -. .-... .-.- .--. -. -.. -.. / - ..- / -.- .-. .-... --- -.. / ...- --- .-.. /
--- ... .- / ..- -.- .... ..- .-. .-..- .-. ... I want my world at the same point
to become smaller and smaller and larger and larger—to be both very small and large as it—as we—are—the scales moving as we go—as we are. And to stop death.

But first and last right here—head over side of rail peering through the bars—I want my world. -.-- -.. / -.-. -.-- .-- / --- -... --. ... .-- -.-- - - / -.... --- .-. .-. .-- .-. .-- ... .-- --- ... .-- -.. / -. . .-... .-.-.- / ..-. .--. / --- -... --. ... .-- .-- -.-- - - / ..-. .-- --- -... -. .. .-- - - . -... / --- / .-.. -. --- - / -.-- -.. / -.-. .-.-. .-- / -- ..- .-- -.. / ..- -.. .-- .-- --. --- --. .-.. .-- .--- - - .-.-.- / [Exit. Alarums.] .-- ..- ... ..- / --- -... / -. .-.-- -.. / --- / -.-. ..- - - -... --- / / ..-. .-.-. / - --- --. .-... --- -.-. / ... .- - -.. --- -.. .-.. / .-- -.-- ..-. .-. / -.... ..- -... -.. - -.. .-.-.- / [Low march within.] --- -... / --. -.-. .-. ..-. ... ..- -... / -.-- / --- -.-. .... ..- --. -.-. .-- . ... / --- / ..-. .-- / -- -... --- - -... -. -.-. - .-.-. / --- .-. / --- -... / - -.-- / - -... --- ..- - / -.-. -... / .-- -.- ..-. / -.-- -.. / -.-. -... / .-.-. ..- -.. ... . - .. . / --- .-.-. / --- / - --- -.-. .-... --- -.. / --- / ... --- .-- ..- -.. -... .-. - - .-.-.- / ....- - / --- -... / .-.- / - - --- ..- --- -... / . . -... / .-- / -. .-... / .-.-. .-.-. ..- -.. / - .-.-. / - ..-. -.. / .-.. .-- -.-- .-.. .-. -.-.. .-- - .-.-.- / . / .-... -.-- ..- .-- --- .-.. -.-. .-.-. / --- / -.-. .. -.-. - .-. .. -.. ..- ... .-- / .-- / .-.-.- ..- -.-. -.. -... . / --- . / .-.-. -- --- .-- / -..-. / -.-. .-- --- -.. / .-.-. -... -- --- / -... .-. -.-. --- / - -.-. / ... --- .-- .-. / ..-.
-..- - - -..- --. --. --- ... The form is ba-dum, ba-dum, ba-dum and then dump where "then" bears the off-screen diacritical mark—the terrific, breath-defying expanse of it, sneaking balls to the wall blue falcon into town to bang a local waitress.

Versus the "if" on which history like spittle hangs and the humorless, bureaucratic and needlessly restrictive powers-that-be depend. ..--- --... .-.-. /...- . ... --- . .-- .... .-.-.- / .-.. -. .-.-. --- -.-. / .-- --- .... .-.- / .--- --- . -. / -... . -... ..- / -. .-- -.. --- ... ... --- ... .-- . -.. .-.-.- / . .-.- --- -.. .-.-.- . / Exeunt omnes (bearing torches). --- --- -... -... . / .-- -- -- --- -.. / -. . . -... ..- / -.- -... -... ..- .-.-.- / [Unmuffling.] -.-. ..- / .-. ... . --- -.. ..- .-- .-. -.. --- -... .-- / --- --- / --. . .... .-- / .-- .-- ....-- .-.- ..- / -.. --- . -... .-- / .-.- --- ..- ..- -.- / . - - ... . / --- -.-. .-. .-. -.-. --- -.. .-. .-- -. / -. . --- -... . / .-- -... / -... -.. . .-.. . - ... .-- / -... .--- --- -... .-- .-- .-.. .-.. .-.-.- / -.-. .--- --- --... --- / --- . .-.-. / [Within.] -..- .-- -... .-.-.- / .-- --.. / -.. . -.... .-- / ..- .-- -... .-.. -.-. --- ... .-- / .--- --- .-.-.- . / -.-. --- .-.. Help me build this wall by adding words to it like "it only hurts when I breathe."

The chair stands in its usual place between two half-burnt thoughts.

Help me build this sound. The voices. Expulsions. . .-.. -. . -.. -.- / -.-. --- ....-. --- -... . --- / -.-. --- .-.. / . --- / -.. --- -... .... ..- -.. .-. ... -..

--- .-.. / ---- -.... --- .-. .... ..- / -. --- .-.. -. / - ---- -.-. -.-. .-.. ..-. .-.. -.-. ... .-.- /
-.. --- -.-. --- -... -- ..- -.. --- -., --- --. / -. . -... ..- / .. -- .--. .-. --- -... -... .
---- -.. / -- --- .--. .-. .-.. .-.- / - . .-.- .-.- -.-. --. .-. ..- / .. .-.. .-.. --- / -- . -.. .-. .-. ..- / -...
..- -- --- -... ....- / .... --- -.. ..... / - ---- I like what everyone is doing
and not doing in circles touching each other, with words mostly.

The preparatory stage requires such—the efforts of care-
fully self-selected people of strong character able to keep great
secrets—and if necessary carry them to their graves. They must
have an extraordinary capacity for self-control and sacrifice. ---
-.-. .--- ..- -.- .-.. -..- --- -.- / -.- --- -.. .-.. .-.. --- / --.. . -.. .-.-.- / [*Enter
the* Players *with recorders.*] .--- --- -... -... . / .-.. -. . -.. ..- / -.-. ..- ...
--- -... -... . .--- -.- / ..- .-.. --- / -.-. .-. --. . .--- -.- / .-.. -. . .-.. ..- / --- -... /
-.-. .... . .-.. - --- .--- .-.. ..- --- .-.- / .--- -. .--- ....- / ..-. -.. --- --. .--- / ..- --.
.-.. --- / --- -- --- / --- --- . - .... / ..- --.. .-. .--- / -.-. --- -.. .-. ..- .... / ..- --.
.-.. --- / --- .-. --- / . --.. / -.-. ..- -.... .-. --- -... / - ..- / . -.- -.-. .... --- -- .-.
--- / -.-- ..- ... . / .--- --- -.. .-. .-.. -.-.. . / .... --- .-. -.. -... --- .-.. -.- --- -.. /
-. ..- -- --- -... -... ... --- -.-. . .-. .-.-.- / .--- --- -.. .-.. / --- / .-.. ... .-- -.... .-.. ..- / .
--.. --- -.. ..- --. --- / - . .-.-. . Daddy, don't go down to darkness today.
--. .-- ..- ... .- -.. / --- -.... --. ....- .-. --- - - / --- / .-.. -. ---- / ..... -.- .-..
/ -.... .-.. -.-. -.-. -- / .-- ..- - . / .-.. ..- -.... ..-. ..-. --- -... . .-.- ... / - - .. ..- ..-.
--- - --- -.. ..- / --- -... -.- -.... / --- -- ..- -... .. .-. --- -.. .-.-.- / [*She falls upon
her bed, within the curtains.*] .-. --- ..- .... --- -.- / --- -... / -.-. -... ..- .
.-. -. . --- -.- / --- / .-. -... --- .-. ..- -.... .-. --- -... .-. -. . / -.-. -... / .-. .-. --- ..- .... /
..- -.- / .-.. --- -... .-. . . --- -.. / .-. -. .-. -... --- -... / .-. -. ..- -... .- . - . - - . --- -..
/ -.-. .- -.- -. - / --- -... . .-. ..- . .... .-. - . / -.-.- / .-.- / .-.. --- -.. / --- -.- ..- -...
.-.. -. . ..-.- The heart stopped.

That's good. It can't be got into words.

At the end of the day, moreover, our ultimate model would
have hardly any words or no words at all—just images to prompt
behavior. .-.. -.... .-- -.-. / ... .- -.. ..- --- / -.-. -.. / --- ... --- -.- / ..- .
.... . --- -.- / . / -.... --- . .-.-. / -.-. -.. .-. --- / --- - -.. ..- .-- .-.- - - ..- /
--- ... .-. -.. . / . / -.-. -.. / -. -... .-.- .- .- . / -.-. / ... .- -.-. --- / -.-- -..
--- Like a yellow bird singing, to sign a single note between the
ears to curve, carve, intervolving sound forms within a series

of shattered visages—if we could hold them at once—in time:
A chandelier hung from the ceiling of being. .-.. -... .-- -.-- / ... ...
..- -..- ..- --- - / -.-- -.. / --- ... --- -..- /.. . .... . --- -.-- / . / -... --- . .-.-.- /
[*Knock.*] -.-- -.. --- / --- - -.. ..- .-- -.-- - - -..- / --- ... .-- -.. / . / -.-- -..
/ -. --- ..-. ..-. . / -.-- / ... .- -..- --- - / -.-- -.. --- I have traveled as a
goshawk, and I am a flood across a field, a wave breaking on a
beach.

    I took the form of ivy, the womb of a forest at dawn.

    I have been a light whose name is Splendor.

    I have been a snake.

    There is hope in the trees on account of the holes made.

    Is that a foreigner or a friend?

    I am a fire on a hilltop.

    I have been a word in a book experienced in battle, its crest
a great wave after which its shout comes. ...-- ----- .-.-.- / [*They
swear.*] - ..- . .-- . --- -... -.... ..- -.. --- / . -... -..- - . --- / ..- --. --- -.- . .-.. --..
..- -.. / -- --- -. --- . -... / --- -... -.. --- .... --- His head at that moment
was a 100 scoops and as many flavors of ice cream. The poem of
his skull. Its surface surfeit, or enough. Its lumps. Hills and fur-
rows. (Is the moon waning or waxing?) Touching a black rock.

    Or at the skull's center, surrounded by misinformation, si-
lence surrenders. --- / -- --- / .--. --- -..- ...- -... ..- / -- --- .... --- -.. / .-.
-. ..- -... .-. -. ..- -... / --- / ... -- --- . -... / .-. ..- .-. .-.. .-. ..- / -. ..- .-. ..- / - ..- /
... --- / .-. ..- -.. -... ..- / - ..- / -... ..- .-. -. -. .-. -. ..- / ..- .-. -. --- / . .-.
..- .... / -.-. -.-. . / ..-. ... --- -... -.. / .... --- / ... -.- --- -- . ..- -... ..- / .... --- -- -.-.
-.... ..- / .-. . . .. - ... There's considerably more to the operation of a
big con than meets the eyes of even the most jaded observer, par-
ticularly if he or she may think contact with the grift's limited to
merely eyeballing a script (a false externality).

    That's because even as we may take in its shape we're being,
PFM, simultaneously taken in.

    Knowing our culpability's essential. For there's no remove.
The con's got no outside. Period. Full stop.

    Over which, like a turnstile, we retch.

Moreover the closer we approach the squeeze—even balled up cowled in sweat at its core—the more we've become its making's part, inc. "-ner." We realize Bravo Zulu an inescapability including resistance's near futility. The con's all FIBUA.

La de da.

At the same time the greater our awareness of our culpability the greater the commensurate punishment, beautifully, the weight of conscience (shame) inflicts. The con's retribution is self-inflicted, self-correcting and self-governing, marginalizing and, ultimately, incapacitating in one way or another undesirable elements.

TLAR.

Or a virtue—conscience, the beginning of real consciousness—becomes a curse, and then we either consciously suffer its prick, which seems contra natura—according to the laws of the con itself—or we put the ECP blinders back on and must become, as she writes, "connoisseurs of boredom."

But everything those people do is aimed at keeping the dial flat at zero. .-. --- -.. ..-. --- -... .-.. / .-.. ..- ... . / --.- -..- ..- / .... ..- .... / .--- ..- -..- ..- .. ..- .... / -. --- -- -- ..- ... / ...- . .-. --- -..- -... ..- ..- ..- / -.. ..- / .... ..- / ....- -... .-. ..- ..- -... .-.. / ... --- -... .... -..-. --.- -..- ..- / ..- ..- / -.-. . ..- -.. / --- .-. . .-. --- -... .. ..- ... ..- / --- ... ..- -... . ... / ..... .-.- -... / ... ..- ... / .-. .- --- ... --- -.. / - ..- / ... --- / -.-. .--- . .-.. ..- ..- -.. ..- / -- --- -... .-. ... .- .. ..- .... / - / -. . ...- ..- -... .-.-.- / [Exit (above).] -- ..- -- ..- / ..- -.. / -..- -.. / .-. ..- ..- ... / .-.- ... --- . ...-.. / .-. .-. --- -... . / ..- .-... -... --- -- / ..- -.-. .... --- ..- ... --. ..- --- -.. ..... / ..-. ..- -- ..- ... ..- .... / .- ..- .... / .-.. -.. / .-. ..- / --.- -..- ..- / ...- --- -.. .. ..- / -. ..- -... .. .-. ... .- .- ..- / -.. .-. -.. / --- / -- --- / -- --- .... --- -.. How many times and ways can this begin—because this poem can never end? .... ..- -.. ... -- --- - -- -.. / - .- ..- ..- / --- .... .-.. ..- ..- -.. .-. ..- --- -.. / - ..- .... .-. -... ..- --... --- / -. ..- -.. ..- -... ..- -.. .--. . .-. ..- -... . .-.- .-.- / [Tearing off his clothes.] --- / -. --- -.. .- -.. --- / -- ..- -.. - . .-. --- / -.. .--. ..- .- ... --- .-. -.-- / [Stabs him.] ..- / --- ... / ... --- - --- ... / --- / -.-. --- -.. - -. --- / --. -.... --- -- --- / -... --- .-. .- -.-. ..- / - -. --- / .-. -... / .- .- --- ... -. ..- --- / --.- -..- ..- / .-.. -.. / .--. --- -.-. ..- ..- / ....- / .-... ..- .-. .... .-. .... --- Know the terrain, avenues of access and egress—ways in (the prime) and ways out end again.

Are there possibilities for rapid maneuver and where do I hide? To hide me—to bed meaning—i.e. "LoØoØoL!" --.- -..- ..- -- / .... ..- / --- .-.. -... ..- ...- ..- / --.- -..- ..- / --- -.- .... --- -- / -.. --- / .-.- -.- -... ..- --.. --- / - --- / -- --- .... .-. -.- .... . .-.. . - --- - ..- / -.. --- / .-. --- .... . .-. --- --- / ...- ..- -... .-.. . .-. --- ... "Do I get nervous? Scared? Sure, why shouldn't I?

"One of the things that gives me a fine feeling of security is to think constantly of problems that may arise. Lapses. Minor details. That way when the moment of decision arrives everything is easier." ..- / - . --.. ..- -... / --.- -.- ..- / --- / -. --- -- ..- -- / ..- / -..- -- / -.-. --- .-.- -.- ... --- - --- -... .-.- / .... ..- / -..- --- / .... ..- -... / .-. --- -- --- / .-.. --- - --- .... / ..- .... ..- .... / .... --- --- / .-. --- - --- / --. -... ....- / - --- / ..-. --- -... .-. .-. -.- -.. --- / ..- / --- -- --- .-. . --- - --- / .-. .-. --- -... / ..- ... ..- .-. .-. / [Enter a Messenger.] -. --- / --- / ..- -... -.- - . .-. .. --- / .-. .--- .-. --- .-. ... / .-. .-. --- --- / .-. .-. --- ... --- / - ..- / --- -.. -... --- -.. .-. / .-.. -.-- / .-. .-. -.. - - --- / ..... / --- -.-. .... ..- --.- -.- -.. --- I am glad to report fleeting pleasures remain the emboweled native. The diversions of direct perception, say, which the arts in part frame—though largely co-opted. Sex, its co-relative, is possible still for the gifted few—and why it's ringed off by prohibition and taboo.

Though even here money casts its eerie glow.

Emotions too may sometimes form unclouded, as known in conscience, but in the main they're quickly circular slung.

Or nature may be free and found anywhere, for all the con's sought to segment and sap it, but such discovery requires an equivalence in mete that's largely forsook.

Hodehum.

And then there's what of which we cannot speak.

Again, however, these experiences prove glancing at best, and it's back to life. Back to duality. A pink mist.

KITDAFOS. --- -.. ....-. -. .-.. / ..- . ..- --- ... ..- -... / -- . .-. .. ..- / --- ... . / ..- . -.. ..- ...- -.. / -- --- --- . / . .-.. / -... ..- ...- . . . ..- / ..... .-. ... ..- -. .-. -.. / . .-- ..- -..

-.. / --- -.,- .-. -. / . .-.. / -.- .-- / .-.. .-.. -...- / --. .- -... .- .-. -. .- .-.. .-.-.- /
[*Enter boy with wine and tapers.*] -.- --- -- -- / --. .. .- -. / -- . .-.. / -- .
-... .-.-.- / [*knocking.*] --. .. .- -. / -.-. .-. -... ..... .-. -. / ..... .-. --- .-. .-. .- -..
/ .-- --- / - . .-- .... / .-.. .- -... ..... --- -... ... .- / .-.- -... .- .-. ... / --- -... ....
/ .-- .- ....- .-. / - .-.- -... .-.-. .- / ..-. ... --- . ... / - .- .. .- .-- ... . .- .-. ... / .-.-
--- .-. .-.- --- -... - When we close on the line, it wavers. We waver.
   Or we've seen the enemy, and it is the monster at the end of
the rainbow.
   "Be still!" ... ... -.. - / .--- ... .- . ... -.. / -- ... -.. ..... .-. -. / --. ... -.. .-. --.
/ - .--- .... / -- --- -.. / -... . .-.. .-. .-. / --. ... .-.- / .- .-.. .-. .- -- / --- -... .. -..
.- -.. / --.. .-. / .- .- -. ... .- . .-. .- -.. / - .- -... ... ... / .--- --- ... .- / . .- - ...
... / --. ... --- .-. ... .- -. ... .- -.. / .- ... -- / ... .- --- -.. / - ... .- -.. / -- ... -.. ....
. -. ... ... -.. / --. .- -.- / ... .- .- .- -.. / -- --- --- .- .- .- ... .- / .-- ... - .- -.. .- .
/ - . .- / --. --- .-. .-. .- .- .- -.. / .... .- ... .-.. ... --- ....- -.. .-.-.- / [*Music
plays. Enter two or three* Servants *with a banket.*] -- --- .-. .- .- .. .- -..
/ .... / - --- .... / ... .- ... .- ....- .- . .-. -. / ... .- . -.. / --. .- ....- ...- .-.
... .- .... / -- ..- .- -. -... / --- ... . / - ... - -... / -- --- -... .. -.. / - --- ... . / ... ...
/ --. . ... .- .-. .- .-.- / [*Whispers in 's ear.*] ... --- .... - .. / .... /
-.- .- .- .. .. / ... .- .-. .... -- -- ... .- -. .- ... / .... --- -.. / --. ... .- --- -..
.-... . .-. / --- ... -. .- ... .- / .- . .- .. .- .- / .-. .- .-. -. ... .- .- .-. -.- --- ... .- ... / ... .- --- -..
/ ..... .-. . . ... .-.. .- ... -.. . . .- / .-- ... ... - ... This never happened. --..
-.. --- .-.- .- --.. / .--- ... .- A mission's a church, and albeit we may
be in different rooms—or compartments—the events are fluid
and our words wide and open limits in which we fit the gap the
world grows from—groans from—so best keep still.
   Bareheaded the gods open a floor of spiders. ..... . --. -.. .- --- -...
. / --.- .-.- . .-.. - . / . .-.. / ... .- .-. --- ... .- --- .... / -- . / .-.- ... .- -... .- .- --- -.. .
/ .... / .-. .- .-.- --- -.. ... ... --- / . .-.- .-. --- -- .. .. / .-.- .- .- ... / . .-. .-.- .-. --- -..
--- .-.-.- / [*Cry within*: "Help! Help!"] .-. ... .- -... ... .- .- / --. ... . /
-.. .- --- -- .. . .-... / --- -.. -- --- -.. ... ... / ..- ..... .-. .- .-. --- -... ..... / --- ... ... --- / -.-.
--- .-.- .- ... ... --- --. ... . --- Each letter of the alphabet is a different war
position. The letter "A" is a ready soldier with legs splayed and
arms akimbo—"B" the grenade grip. "C"'s a warrior ring, its gap
where the enemy is led in to close on "O" where victory's roar, a

sullen dance over nowhere, resounds.

And so it goes, row on row forming, scattering and reforming, marching words linked to captive joys, promises, that as they appear crumble and recede: So much more "fodder of capitalist motor wash demented statecraft fed to zombie horde." ..- /

-.. --- -.. / .... --- .-. .-. .-. --- -.. .-.. --- -... ..- / .-. .-. -.- .-. .-.. .-. ..- / ... ..- / -- .

-.. --- .-. .-. ..- .-.-. / - --- -... -- . -... ..- / .... -.- / - . / ..- .... --- / ..- /

.... ..- / .-. / .-. -. ..- / . / -.. ..- .- . .-. / ....- -.. --. .. .-- .... --- ... --- -- ..- -..

.-.. ..- / .-. .- --- --. .... . --- .-. --- / ... --- -... --- / ... --- / --. --- ... --- / ....

..- -.. --.. --- / -... ..- .-. .-. .-. --. -. .. --- -.. .-. .-- Everybody is running

around. Don't look there. ..... .-. -.... .-. .-. .-. --- .-. .- / - .-. .. . . .-. .. -..- -..

/ --.- -.- --- - / ..... / -- . ...-. ..- -.. -.. .-. .-. -.- -.. / ..... -.- .-. .-- --- -.. / .-. .--

-- / --- -.. ..- --- / ..- .-. .. / .-. .-.- -- / .-. .-. -.... --- .- . --- --- / ..... --- -.. .-.

--- -.. / .-. .. ..-. --- .-. .-. --- -.. / .-. .-.-- -- / .-. .-. ..- -.. .-. ... --- / ..- .-.

/ .--. --- ....- .-.. / .-. .-.- -- / .-. .. . .-. .-. --- -.. / --- - / --.- -..- --- -...

-..- -- / -.... ..- .-.. .--- / ..- --.. --- / --- -.- .-. ..- -- / -- . ... -.- ..... / .....

-..- -- "Goddamit to hell, what the hell happened?" .-.. --- ... --- -...

/ .-.. -. .-.- / -. ..- -... -... --- / --- .-. -. ..- . .-.. ..... / ..-. -.. --- / -. .-.- --.

--- -.. / ..... --- ... -.- / .-. .-. -. .-.. -.. / .-. --- .-.. -. Even now a rocket

zooms towards Mars. -- -.. .- -... .-. --- / --- / --.- -.- . ..- -.. / ... --- /

-- --- -.. --- / - ..- / .. - .-- --- -.. - / .-. .- -.- -.. .- .. .-. .- / .-- .... . -- . ---

-- .... / -. . --.. --- / -- --- .-. .-. --- -.. / .-. -. -. . ...-. / -- .- ... --- -.. .....

--- -.. .-. -.- / --.- -.- -.. / .... ..- / -. --- .-. .-. .... --- / .--- -.- ..... .-. --- .-. .-. /

.... ..- / .-. .-. . . --- / --.- -.- ..- / .-. .- ..- ..... --- .- .-. / --.- -.- --- / -.-. .

..- -.. / ... --- / .-. ..- .- ..- --- / ..- .-.- ..- / ..- / . -.. ..... .-. --- / .-. .-- --- ..- /

.-. ..- --- --- / ..... -.- / - .- ..... .-. --- -.. .-. ..- ..- -.. .-. ..- --- / --- ... .-. .-- --- .-.-.- /

As scoped, we can never leave the con. Rather, most of what we are is in the game, awash in slosh.

We're grown through its enmeshings, like a tree around a fence (law) built to confine it—with "fence" in this sense both swag trade and what defines and confines fobbit farmers. We can't see the con because areas that are in play are obscured and/or absorbed like a pink cloud into our own criminality.

Or crime's seeded into language as corporal imagery itself is codified by its warp: Or in language we can't simultaneously maintain awareness of what's forward opening and behind closing—or vice-versa—though fire we know has neither front nor back.

GOFO.

The very conceptual structures on which the con's framed, including the grammar by which these words are rendered intelligible, are soaked in its dance.

And their sole aim: to separate us. .-.. --- - --- / ..- .... .-.. --- / .--. -... --- -.. .-.- -.. .-. . --- - --- / .-. --- -.. / --- ....- -.. .-.. --- / ..... -..- --- ...- .. .-.-.- / [*Enter three or four* Servitors.] -- . -... --- - --- / .-.. -... --- -.. .-.- -..- . .... --- .-.-.- / .... --- .... / -.... --- - . ... --- .... / ....- / . -.. .-. .... . -.. --- / -. .-.- -- -- . .... - ..- -.. .-. .-. .. ..-.- / ....- / .-.-. -.- - --- / -.. --- / .-.. --- -- -.. / .-.. -... -.- -.. -.- --- / .-. .- --- -.. / .... --- .... / -.... .- -.-. ..- ... - .. .... / - .. -- . -. .... --- .-- / - ..- / .-.. --- -- -- .-- ..- / .-. .- --- -.... .-. .-.- . --- - -.. / .... --- - / .--. ..- --- -.. ..-. .-.-.- / .-. .- --- / -.- .- ..- .-.- / -.. ..- -.. / ....- / . .-.. .-. .... --- / .-. .- --- -.... .-. .-. / .--. ..- --- -.. / .-. .- --- -.... .-. / --- / -.. .-. .... ..- -.. / -.. .... -.. / ....- / . .-. .-. .... . .-. / .-. .- --- -.... .-. / .-.-. ..- -.... ..-. .-.- --- -.. .-.- .. --- -.. .-. .-. . --- - -.. / - ..- / --- .-. .- ..- .-.- -.. --- / ..- -.. / -.... ..- -.-. .-.-.- . .-.. --- / -. .-. -..- -.. -.. .-. .-.. He began to cry. He butted a guard in the eye. .-.- ..- -... / - ..- ....- -.. / --- ....- / ..... --- / -. ..- . ... / ..... .-. -. / --- .... .-.. ..- .-.. / ..... .-. -. -. / .-.. .- --- - .... .-. -. / .-.- .-. -..- -.- .-. .-. / --.. -..- / .-. -.- .-. -.- .-. .-. -..- / -..- .-. -. / .-.-. .-. -.-. / . -.-. / -- . .-. .. / ..- . - .-. ..- --- -- / -- --- .-.. -.. .-. .-. . .-. .-. ... / . ...-. -. . .-. .-.. / ..... .-. -. -- --- .-. .-.. .-. .-. / -- . .-. . .-. / ..- . . - .-. ..- .... / .-. . --- -.-. .-. / . ...-. -. .-. .-. --- -... ... .-. .-. / - ..- .-. --- ... .-. .-. ..- / . .-. . --- - / .-. -.-. ..- .... -. ..- ..- -.-.- / .-. --- ... .-.-.- / .-. .- --- -.... *They put him in the tomb.* -..- -... - / -- . .-. .-. / - ..- .-. -.. / --- -..- . .-.- -... .-. / ..- -.. / ....- -... .-.- - ..- .-. .-. / ....-. / --.. .-.- -.- .... -.- .-. -.. .-. .-. -.- / --- -... .-.-.- / .-. .- --- -.... -.... ..- -.. Though alternate views are possible without shear, the surest path to solving the complex, technically demanding challenge of getting a grip is to remain perfectly still—even as such might cause one to be ill. -.... ..- .-.. .- --- -.... .-. .-.- / . .-. .... .-. .-.- .-.- / ....- ..- / -... .-. / - -.-. -.... .-. .- --- -.... .-. / .-.-. / -- .-. .-.. -.... .-. --- -.... -. .. .... / .-. --- / -- .-. -.... .-. .... -.. -.- . .... / .-. --- . / -.- .-. -.... .-. --- -... .-.- . .... / .-. -.- .-. -.-.- / *Enter the* Clown *with a basket, and two pigeons in it.* .-.- ..- -- -- --- .-.-.- / .-... ..- -- -- --- .-.- -.. .-.-.- / .-... ..- -- --- .-. -.. .-. .-.-.- / -.-. --- -. --- -.. .-.-. . --- -... .-. .-.-.- / [*Exit Messenger.*] - --- -.. / .... ..- -.-. .-.- . -.

/ .-. ..- .-. --- .-.. / -.-. ..- -... -.-. --- -.. . .-.. --. / .... . --- -. .-.. .-- --- /
.... ..- -.. --. --- -.. / --. ..- .... . .-.. / -.. .-.- --- / - ..- .-.. .-- --- -.- --- -.. / -.-.
--- .-- --- -. / -- --- .-.. .-- / ..-. --- .-.. .-- --- ... / -- ..- -... ..- .-.- --- .-.-. / -.-.
--- .-- --- -. -.. .-- .-- --- / -.-- --- -... .. -. / - --- -.-. .. / .-.. .-- .-. . .-. .-.. / -- ..- -...
..- -.- --- / -.-. ..- -... --. .. ..- --. . --- ..... DHKOKATHHITBOTB. -- ---
..- -.. / .-. . .-- / -.-. -.. / - --- - / --- / -. .-.- - / . -... / - --- -.. -.. -.. --- -.. /
-.-- -.. / .-. --- ..- ... / ..- -.- / -.-. -... --- -.. / -- --- -... / -.-. -.. . . -..- Word
chords fragment. Break. Hang back. Call. They have sad faces,
upturned in their splash sites.

To work with those shards and in a wilderness of monitors
make a wall of winds. Movement. Peepholes.

To organize a moment.

How to perfect the moment, its fierce shine—cut fire to
forms in which an effect may take hold, HOCOWS, across a
red tablecloth, to gauge what remains: a square frame structure
perched in the center of the roof of the main building built from
nine different materials (noun, pronoun, [adjective], verb, ad-
verb, participle, [preposition], conjunction, interjection). .-.. ..- /
- ..- --. .--- -.- --- -... / ..... -.. / ..... / --- .-.. --- / .-.. ..- / .-.. -... --- -.- ---
.... . -.. / ..- / .-.. ..- / .-. .... ..- .- He put them into the bag last.

The whole thing—a small, rounded, clearly demarcated sen-
tence—took about 30 seconds. --. ..- .... -.-. -.. . - -. ..- . .-.. / . ...-.. /
--- -..- .-.- .-. -. / - ..- -... / -. ..- -... -... / ..- -.. . / .-- --- .... / ....- / .- --- -.-.
..- -.. Nobody knows what handholds may happen under a table.

"But we can't see there from here... going forth with torches
to fetch back fire from hell... to light our way ahead..." she sang,
her fractured face on one elbow squinting out one eye through a
whiskey bottle on the piano—at the dawn, which was the color
of it.

Raft of the sun splintered over the mountains.

Playing something sad and soft to nobody listening. --- ..-. .-..
..- -.. / -. ..- / .-- --- .... / ..- -.. .-- -. .-- .... -.-. ..- - / . .-.. / .-.. -. --- .-.. / .-..
.-- --- .... .-.. ..- .- .-. / .-. .-- --- ... .- - / .-.. -. -. ..- / -.-. --- -- -.-. --- --- --- -..
..- We cop to any sop—in fact will pay dearly for it—KITDA-

FOS—rather than face the hole. And the more outrageous the better. It makes life biting.

But fangs stuck in floorboard, we bite Bravo Zulu only ourselves. --. ..- -... - . .-.. --- -... -.. .- -- / -- --- -.. .-.- / .-.. ..- -.. .- .... ..-.- / *Enter* Messenger. -. --- -- --- / ..- .... .-.-.- / .-. ... --- -- --- .-.. / --- -...
.... / - ..- .-. --- -... .- -- / .-.. .-.- .- -- -.-.- / .-.. --- ... -- / ..-. .... ..- -.. .-.
..- .... .-.-.- / ..-. .- -... -.. --.. .... / --- .-. . -. .. / .-.. .-.- --- / . -- .-.. --- -... .- .-.
--- -.. .-. / ..-. .-.- -.. --- --- .... / . .-.. -... .-. --- .-. .-.-.- .... / -.-.
..- .... .-. . --- ..- .-.-.- / [*To* Servants *within.*] -- -..- ... . ..- -.. / .... .-.-.
..- .-. . / --- .... --- / .... .-. . ..- .-. . ..- -- / -. --- -- . -.. . .... .-.-.- / ..- ..- ...
/ .-. .- .-. -.- -.. .... / ..- .-. . / -- --- ... ..- -.. / .-. --- -.. / ....- -.. .-. . -.. -- /
.... - . ..- .-. .-. -.- -.. .... .-.-.- / ..- ... . / -- ..- / .-.. --- -.. .-. . ..- .. . .-. . / ..-.
-... ..- . .-. .. .-. -- . -.-.- / .-. -... --- / ..... --- .-. -.. .-. .-.- --- / --- / .-. .- .-.-.- --- / -.
.... .-.- --- ... . . .-. . --- -.. .- / - ..- .-. . / -- --- --- .- ..- .... .-. / --- .-. .-. ....
--- -... .- .- -- / -... --- -... .-. . ..- -... .-. / -.- .-.- ..- -... -... "There is no god but
strife wrapped in a sod."

The population grows, or "proliferates."

In the windshield is a bullet hole. A dick holster. ... --- / -- ..-
--. / -.-. ... . / .-.. --- .-.. .-.- .-.-.- / .... --- / -- ..- --. / -.-. ... . / ..... --- .-..
.-.. / .-.. .... / - ---- - ..- -.. .-.-.- / .-.- ..- --. / ..- -.. / ... .-. -.- -.- ..- .... .-. . --.
.-.-.- / .... --- -- / - -.- / ...- . ..- .-.-.- / -. .- -- -.. / - ..- .-. / ....- . -.- .-.-.-
.- / [*Embracing.*] .--- ..- --. / ... . / ..... . / -.- .--- --- -.. / --. .-.. --- .-..
.-. / ..- -.. / . .-. -.- .- ..- / --- .-.-.- ..- .-.. / . / -- --- -... -.. --.. ..- -.. I limit my
ideas to basic classical themes—man, animal and a little bit of landscape.

It sounds boring, but I've found in these three subjects all the madness in the world may be found. - ..- .-.. / ..- -... / -.-. --- -.... ..- /
..- -.. / -.-. ... ..- .-.-. / -.... ..- ..-. .... ..- .- -.- ..... .-. --- --- -.. / --- ..- / .-. -.. -..
-.. ..- -.. / --- ..- / .-. -.-. --- ..- .-. -. ..- .-. -.- / .-.- .-.-.- / ..- .... -... --- .-. ..- .-.-
.-.-.- / -. ..- .-.. ... .- -... / ..- -.. / - ..- .-. .- / .-. -.- -.- ..- / --- .-.. / ... --- -...
-.- Words meeting and parting again to meet and part again and
again out ahead—what came before words, before wine, before
the goddess.

Darkness and terror.

"Be still!" ..- ...- .- -.. .. -- .. -.. .-.. .... / .-. --- -.. .-.. .-.. .-. -.. .-.. .-.. / - .- / .... ..- / - .- -... --- -.-. .... ..- -... / .... --- / .-.. ..- -.. -... .... ..- -.- -... / - ..- -.. -.. .-.. ..- .-. -.... . ...- Between the lines the sun rhymes. - ..- -.-. / --- / --- -... - ..- -. / -.-. -.. .- ..- / -.. .- --- --- / -- ..- / -- --- .-.. --- -..- / -.. ..- .... --- / -.- -.. . --- --- / - ..- ... .- -.. . --- / .... .. -... / -. .- -- . .... -. --- - --- / .-. -.. --- -... -.-. -.-. ..- / ..- .... / .... ..- / .-. --- .... --- -..- / .-. --- - . --. --- / --- -.. .- .... ..- .... / - ..- / -- --- -.-. ..- -.. .-.- / [A knock.] .-.. ..- -- --- --- / -.-. -.-. ..- / .... ..- .-.. --- -.-. / ..- / --- . -.. . - --- / --- .-. .-. --- -- / --.- -.. -.. ..- / -.- -.. -... --- --- / - ..- ...- ..- / .-. --- -- --- / .-. ..- ..- -- / ..... . --- / .-. ..- ..- -.. .-. .-.. --- - --- / .-.. -- -- / -. .-. --- -- ..- -- / .... --- -.. .-.. .-. --- .-.-. / .-. --- -- --- / -.- -.-. .-.. --- -. . -... / ..- -.- - / .- ..... .-. .-. --- -.- / .-. --- ... --- -.-. -.- / --- .-. .-. ..- / .- ..- .-.. / --- -.. .-. --- -.. .-.- - -.. / --- -.. .-.. .-. --- .-. -... / --- -... / ..- .-.. ..- .. .-. --- / .... ..- . .-. . -.-. / .. -... .- -... -.. .-.- --- / -- ..- / -.... ..- - . -- . - .... Even primitive man felt a horror of human beings murdering each other. They shrank back, as though touching fire. And then drew closer.

But there must have been music in those caves, something to "dance around," she went on to exclaim. --- / -.-. -.-. ..- .... / - -..- / --- -... / .... -.. ... -.-. -.-. / --- .-.. ..- .-. / .-. ... --- / . -.. / .-.. .-. --- -. -.-. --- -.. / - - ..- .... -.-. ..- - ... --- -.. ..- --- / -- --- -.. ..- .-.-.- / Exeunt. .-- --- --- --. / -- . -.. -.. .... / ..- -.. / --- .-. .-.. --- .-. ..- .- .- .-. --- -.. ..- / --- -.- . .-. / -.... -.- -.. -.. .-. .-. / -. -.... / -. --- -.. / -.-. --- -... We treat the world like a rental car. .... --- - -- / .... ..- -.. .-. .-. / .--- --- -- / -.. -.-. .-. .- ..- .- .-. / --- ..- - / --- ..- ..- .- -.. ...- --- ... - . --. .--. / . / .-. ..- -.. -- --- .... . -.- --- / --- -... -. .-. --- / --- ..- -. .- .-.. ..- -.-. ...- ... --- ... . . / .-. --- -.-. ..- --- ....- ..- / --- ..- .-. .-. .-.. -.-. .-. .-. ..- .-. -.. -.. ..- ..- -.. Emergency is a direct means of response which leaves no room for thought, doubt (the dwindling). It is reflex without perspective, act without shadow and high-noon durable jelly sans distance: the blade on its end over the pupil of the eye ready to punch the black hole home. -.-. .-.. -.. -.. --- .... ..- -.. -.... .-.. -. -.. / --- -.. ... / --- -.-. -.. --- -.-. -.. .-.. .... .-. ..- .-.. ..- -.. .... --- / .-.-. / ... ..- -.-. .-. ..- --- / ..- -.. --- -.... / -. .- --- -.. .... / -.-. -.-. ..- .... .. -.. .- .. .- ..- .-. .-. / -. .- --- --- - ..- / ..- -.. --- .... --- / .. .- ... --- -.. ..- - ..- / -.-. -. .-. --- -.... .... / -. --- --- -.. / --- -- / .-. -. .-. --- / -.-. ..- -.-. -.. ..- .-. .-. .-. .-. / --- -.-. -. . / . / -. --- --- -.. .... / -... .-. .-.-. / --- --- -... ..- ... ..- .- .-. ..- .. ..- / -.-. -.. .-. .-. . -.- / ..- .-. ..- / .... ..- -.-. --- --- ... / -. .-. .-. -. --- --- - --- /

-. --- -.. --. - ..- She sent forth her frenzied cry, her heart immense and unending foaming with the blood of harvest aflame with the smell of mown grasses.

Or was it a song?

Who knows? A song most likely she rode out of the unknown to nowhere.

Rockets boomed and novas exploded into galaxies, but she didn't hear them. It was the call of the migrating cranes overhead that drove her on. --- .-. .-. --- -.-. .-.. -... ..- - / -.- -.-. . -.. / -- . -.. --- / -... --- -- --- -. .-.. . / .--- --- / -.- --- .... .-. . / -. .--- --- -.. .-.. --- / .... ..- -.-. -... --- .- --- .- -.. .-.. / -... .. -.. / -. --- -.. / .-.. .-. .- . .-.-.- / *Kneeling.* .-.. --- -... -... ..- -.. .-. / -.- --- -... .-.. .-. -.-. . / .--- --- / .-.. ..- . / -- -- ..- / -.-. -.-. .-. .-. .- .-.. / -... .. -.. ..- .-. --- .... / .--- --- -.. -.. ..- / -. ..- . / .-. ..- .-. --- .- / .... -.- -... .-.. .-. --- --- .- -.. / .--- --- --- / --- . -.- .-. -.- .-. -. .-. --- .- / .... -.- -.-. - --- -- .- -.. / .-. .. ..-. .-. --- .- .-.-. / -- -.- -.. .-. .-. .-. --- / ..- -.- .-. -... / .-. -.- .-. . . - / .-.. .-. --- .- .... ..- -- -- ..- / -.- --- -. .-. .-. --- / -... .. .- -- .... / .-. .-.. --- / ..- -. -. . -.- --- ..- --- / .-.. -.- .-. . - --- .- .-. .-. .-. ..- / -.- .-. -. .-.. .-.. -.- .- ..- -.- / -. ..- .-. .... .-. . / .... --- -.... -... .-.. / --- -.-. -.-. ..- .-. -.. / .-.. ..- --- . / .-. ..- .-. .-. .-. --- --- -.- .-. -.-.-. / *[Giving a paper.]* --- ... ..- -.. / .-. -.-. ..- .... .-. --- .-. .-. / -.-. -.-. .-.. -. / .... -.- .- -... . / .- ..- .... . / .... ..- .-. -.-. -.-. . .- -.. / --- .- .- .-. .. --- / --. .- ..- -. / .-.. .- -.. / -.- .- ..- -.- ..- -.-. .- -.. .-. -.-. / .... -.- --- .... / .-. -.-. --- ....- --- / -. .--- --- -.. / .-.. ..- . / .... --- . Even he'd been an idiot, adorned with tasks. A necklace of skulls. .-. . / .... . --- -- --- / ... .- --- .... .-. . -.-. .- --- .-. .. / . -.. / -.-. -... .- --- / -. .... . .-.. --- -.. .-. --- / . -.-. -. ..- / -.-. .-. - -.. ..- .-. --- .- .... . --- / ..- .-. -.. ..- --- / ... --- / .... -..- .-. --- / -.- .-. ..- .-. --- .- .- .-. -.- -.- ..- --- The letters in my head (a product of the movies) filled with icy, thick crisscrossing thoughts.

"I've had to make a tremendous effort to keep my personalities, their each ineffable glow, from getting mixed up," she bemoans. - -.- .... .- -. ..- / -- --- .... --- / -.- .-. --- -.. ..- / -.-. -.-. / .... --- -- / -... .. .- . -.-. / .-. .- --- -.- / -.-. -.- / .... --- -- / ..- --- -- / .... . -. -. / --- .-..... .-. / *[They fight.]* -.- --- -.- --- / -- -.- .. --.. .-. --- ..- / .--- .- .... / -.- -.- .- .-. .- -. -.- . -.-. / --- / --- -.. / . - -. / .... . . / -... .- .- .-. / .-. *[Dies.]* ...- --- - . / -- / ...- . - ..- / .-.. --- -. -. .-. / .-. --- -. -. .-. -. . /

.-. -. / -- --- .... --- / ...- / -.- -.. ...- . / .--- ..- - -.. ..- -. --- / -- -..- --.. --- / .-.-.- / --- / ...- .... ..- .-.. -.- -.- / ..... . --- .... .. -.- -.. .... .-.. ..- --- / --- -.. / ..-. --- -.. . / .-- / --- --.. / .-. -.... ....-.- / Knock. --.. --- -.-. .--- .

-- --- ... --- / -.-. -.-- / -- --- / -- -.- --.. . / .--- - ...- --- -.- / - --- ...- ..- -... --- --.. --- ...- --- / .... --- -- . / .... / -- -.- --.. -- ..- -.- / -- --- -- / .-. -. --- -.. / .-. / .-.-.- / --.. ..- / -.-. -.-- / .... --- -- / ..... --- / -- --- ... / --- .-. -.-. -.-- -.-. .-. --- / .--- ..- / -.-. ..- --.. / -.. --- --.. --- .-.-. / - --- -.-. -.-. -... ..- / .-. -..- ..- / .-. . -. / -.. / -- --- .... --- / --- / -.-. ..- ..- --.. .-. --.. ..- .-. -.-. -... .... ..- .- / .-. -.... ..- / .

.-. -. / --.. . ....- --- .-.. -.-- To untangle a knot we need the mind of a line, of a cyclops, clear barrel, flight (a phoenix in).

I've tried to pile the pump and dump high enough to climb to see past myself to the wee hole set off where everything everywhere goes berserk—reach far enough to show just how gone things (properties) are—but am sunk with just my grape poked out. .-..- -. ..- / .-. -. --- -.. ..- .-. ..- .... / --- ..-. / .-. -. --- -.. ..- -.. ..- / --- -.... ..- /

--- .... / ....- / --- .... / --- / .-. -.- ..- .-. .. .. / -. .--- . .-... The puzzle palace resembled the inside of a beehive put together by bees working completely at random. --- ...- ..- .-. / ... --- / .-. .- ..- -... -- .

.... --- -.. / - ..- / -.- --- ..- -... .-. / ..- .-.. / ....- / -.... ..- .... .-. ..- /

--- ... / -.-. -.- -.- -.... .. / ..- .... .-. / -.- -.. / -. -.... --- -- -.. / -. --- -... -. --- -.. /

--- -.. .... ..- .-.-. / [Taking R—'s dagger.] --- . -.. ..... . /

.... --- -.. .-.. / . ... / .-. .... --- -.. .-. .... .-.-. / .-. -. --- -.. .- .... / - .- ..- / -. --- -- -- .- .... /

/ -. -. --- -... .. --- -... -.... --- -.-. ... ..- .. ... .-.-. / .--- ..- / ... .- ..- -.. .... / - ..- / .-.

--- -.... ... ..- -.. / .... --- -. .... / - .- ..- / .-. -.- -.. -.- -.-.- .... --- . ...- ....

/ - ..- / -.- .- ..- -.. -.- ..- .- -.- -.-.- / . ... / .- -.-. ..- --- . .-.. / -- --- -.. / --- -- .

/ ..-. .. . ..- .... .- / ..- -.- .. / .--- -.- -. ....- ..- / .-. -.-. --- -.- .-.. / -- --- . . . .-.-.- /

Exeunt [severally]. -- --- . ..... / .--- --- --- -- ..- .... / ..- --- ....-.. ..... --- -..

- / - . .-.. / .--- -.- .-.. . .... / ..- .-.. ..- --- . .-.. / .--- --- -. -.-. .-.. .-. ..- -.- ..- .-. .-.-. / -.

--- ... .-. -.... ..- -.. ..- -.. / ..- .-. .. / .... --- -- / ..- ....-. / -.- -.. / -. .- --- -- ..- /

-. --- -.. .- -.. --- -... --- -... .- ... ..- .-.-. / Enter a [third] Gentleman. . ... /

--- / --- .-. -.-. .-. --- -... .-.. ..- / - ..- / -.. --- -- -.-. -... ..- ..- ..- / -- --- .-. ....

/ ... --- / -- --- . ..... --- -... / --- / -... --- -- --.- .- The goal's never been to eliminate crime. After all it's the human basis.

But rather, instead of everyone being on their own crime

spree, to centralize and coordinate the process. . ... -....- -- --- -.
--.. ..- -.. -....- - .--- --- -... / .-. -... --- -- -- --. ..- - / -.-. . ... -.... --.- --- -- -.
.-.-.- / .--- --- --. -. .-- -- ... -..- / ..- - . .-.. .-.. . / --. -. --- ... ... / -..- --.. -..- -..
--- / --. -. --- ... ... / --- .-. .-. .-. --- --. ... / -..- .... -.- -... ..- -... .... ..--- /
Enter, with Drum and Colors, C—, [Doctor], *and* Soldiers. -...
..- ... .--- --- -.- --- / .-.. --- / -.- -.- ... .--- -.- -- / -.- -.- ... ... / --- .-. .-. /
.... -.- ....-. --- -.. .-. --- -.- .-. --. / .... .-. --- -.- -.-. -.- . ... .-. / -.- --- -..
.-.. -.... --- / ... -.... --.- --. -. --- -.- .-. --- / -..- / .--- --- .-. .-. .-. .... --- -..- /
. .... .-. --- -.- .-. -.- .-. / --- .-. -.- .-.. --- -.- / .-.. . .-.. --.- . -... / .-.. --- /
-.- -.- ... .--- --- -.- -- / --. -.- --- ... ... -.- --- -.- .-.. . --- / -... .-. / -.-. /
.-.. -.... --- --... --.. --. --- -.. / [*He puts the handkerchief from him, and it drops.*] .--- ..- -.- -.- / .... -.... --.- -.. .-- ..
-.... ..- -.. / .--- . .-.. -.- .. -.-. / -- . .-.. -.. .. --- / -- --- / -.- .-. / -. -.- .-. --- /
....- MMFHATTATAFTSWM. .--- --- --- -- -.-. --- / -.- -.- .-. . .-.. .. -.. .
-- .. .-- --- / . - ... .--- .-. / -.- -.- .-. .-.. --- -.- --- / -.- .-. .-. --- -.-. -. --. ..- .-.- / *Exit*
[*above*]. .-. -. .--- .... -.- / .-.- ... .-.. .-.. -.-. / -... . / -.- .-. --- -- --- / --. .-.- /
-.-. --- .-.-. / --- -. .-.. .-.. .-. --.- --- / --- .-. --- --- .. .. / -.- -.- .-. .-.. --- -.- /
.-- --- -.- . . / -... . / -.- -.- .... -... .- --- -.-.- / -.- --- --- / -- --- --.- .-. --- /
-.- --- .-.. . -.- --- / --. -.- --- -- -.- .. -.- --- ..- .-. / -.- .- --- -.- / .... -.- --- .-. -... / ....
. / -- -.- .-. --- -.- .-. --- / -.- .-. -.- .-.- .-. --- / --- -.- --- -. -.- .-.- . -- .- --- -.-.- / *They*
knock, and T— [*above*] *opens his study door.* -- .- -- --- ... . / .-- .- .. -..
-.- / -.- .-. -.- --- .... --- / .-. -.- .-.. --- -... --- -.- -.- -.- ... / -.- --- -.- -.- ... .- .-.- .-. --- ..- /
-... --- --- / -.- -.- --- -- --- / .... --- --- .... --- / -... .-. -.-. -.- / .-.- -.- --- -.- .... .-. / -.- -.- .
--- / --- --- -.- -.- --- ..- .-. --- .-. --- / -..- . / -... .- . -.- / -..- ... --- / -.. .- --- / .-. ..- .. /
-. -.-- -.- -.-- --- No one knew what the mode of selection had been,
and a certain amount of suppressed curiosity was manifest as we
milled around in a state of rectal cranial inversion trying to act
as if we did.

Or how much do the other guys know I knew I don't know
I knew?

Of course one slim figure completely phenomeniched the
scene. Despite the cold evening, and as if the most natural thing
in the world, she wandered around in nothing but a very white
pair of panties, her blond hair piled on top of her head knotted

Greek-style. --.. ..- ... ..-. .... / --- ... . / -. ..- .-.. / .--. --- .- -... - / .--. . ... / -- ..- / -... .. ..- .-.. / .... .-. -. ..- ... ... - -.. Way. Out. There. Houses. Parked cars. Buttresses. Lives drug and dug in.

I must just chuck them into the model. Get the bastards in.

Why did they say that? Is that some secret ritual they go through?

The careless people.

The ghouls at the edge of the frame.

"Be still!" -- ..- -.. / -- .-- .-.. -.. / - -..- -.. .-.- .-.. / ..... --- -.. .-.. / -- --- -..- / -.. --- -.. / ..... -.-- --- .... / -- --- .-.. ..- ..- -.. .-.-.- / -.- --- -..- .-.. / -.- .-.. ..- / -- / --- .-. -.-.-.- / [Aside.] ---- -- .- / -.. --- -.. / --- -... .-. -. --- -... - / -- / -.-- --- / -.- --- -... .-.. .-.. -- / -- .-- .-.. ..- -.. / .-. ..- --- -.- .-.. .-.. --- --.- / -.. --- -.. / --- .-. -... .-. ..- -- . -. / --- / -- .-. .-.. ..- -.. / - ..- .-. .-. --- -.. .. .. -.. / ..- - .-. .-.. --- -.. / --- .-. . / .-. .-- .- .-.. / .-. ..- --- -.. .-.. .-.- --- -.. / --- -.- / --- -.- / .---- .-.-.- / --- / -- --- - .-.-.-.. .-. --- -.. -.. .. ..- -.. / -.. --- -.. / -.-- --- -.. / .-.-. / -.-. --- -.-- .-.. ..- -.-- / --- -.- / -.. --- -.. / --. .--- --- ... -...-.. / -.-- --- / -.. --- -.. / --... ..- -... ..- -.- / -- .-- .-.. ..- -.. / .-.. ..- .-.- / ..- ... .- / .-. .-.- --- -.- -.. / -. ..- .-. -.-. --- -.. ... --- / -. .-.-.- ..... .-. .. .... -- ..- -.-. -.. .-.. / --- / ....- .-. ... .-. ..- -... --- -.- .-.. .... My god, he didn't have any brains left. .--. -... ..- -- .-.- --- / - ..- / ....- -.-. .... / -- --- -.. .-. --- -... ... ..- .... / -.. / -.. / -. --- -... ... . / ..- -- / -. .-.- -- / - -... --- .-. -. -.-. -- / -... --- ... .-. -. -.-. -. --- -.- -.-.- / [He kills her.] .--. -... --- --- ... .-.- ....- . -... --- .... .-.- -... / . -... ... --- -.. ..... .-.- -.- / .-. --- ... .-.. -.-. -... ..- .... / - ..- / .-. -. -.- -.-. -- -.. .-. --- .-.- -.- / .-. -. --- -... ..- .- ... . --- .... .-.- -.- / .-. -. --- -... -... -... --- ..... .-. --- .... / -- -.-.- . .-.. / .-.. / . -... ..- . --- / - ..- -.. .-.- -.. .-.- .-. . --- -... .. / .-. --- -- / --- --.- .-.- ..- .- .-.. ..- .-.- .-.. / --.- -.-. ..- ..- / --- .... / -.-- .... --- ... .- --- The fresh sheets of copper on the courthouse's new dome will fade to grey green in a year.

The state too fades, and its end when each may rule how each is apart—is the art.

But what about the impaired, delinquent, the loose and shiftless—the rummy and drifter, punk, salvokicker, goofball, goner, deficient, derelict, dufus, doper, hobo, kook, tosser, geek—the cripple and wretch, stranger, budmash, waif, lowlife, and vagrant—those ragmen and outcasts, tramps, oddballs, hopheads, mudlarks, gamins and gamines encamped under the bridge at jungle court roasting roadkill over the firepit?

The sun sets through trees music leaves. ...- .... .-. .. .. / ..- ....
.-. -... --- -.... ... --- .... / -.-. --- .... ..- / ..- -... ..- / --- . -... . --- / --- / ...
-.-. .-. .-. --- / .... .. -... / ...-. ..- . .-.. --- / - ..- / ..- -- -.-. --- ... --- --. ..- -- .-.-
.- / ..- .... .-.. --- -.-. ..- ... ..- .-. ..- / .-. --- -- / ..- .... ..- .... .-.-. / ..- / .-.
--- -... .-. --- / ..- ... ..- / -. .-. --- --- -..- / .... . -... . / --- / -.-. --- -... -.-. ... -.. --- /
--.- ..- ..- / --- .... / --. ..- -.. ..- -.... --- . .... / ..-. .... --- --. ..- -.. -... -... Kick the
tires and light the fuse. ...- ..- -... . .--- -- / .-.. . .-.. . .-.-. / *Enter the*
Messenger *again.* . -. .-. -... --- . .-. -.- --- / --.- -.- --- ..- -... .. .. -... ..- / -....
..- --. .. -- / --.- -.- --- -... -.... -.- -- / -.... ..- .-. -.... --- --- ..- .... ..- -.. .-. --- .-. /
..- ..- .-. ..- .... -.- .... / --.- -.- --- - / . .-. ... ..- / --- -- --- -... Nobody
is afraid here. Life goes on as usual. ..- -- -.-. --- -.... --.- -.-. ..- -- ..- -..
.-. ... . / --- ... ...- / - ..- / ...- -.... ..- - ..- / --- .-. ... ... --- .-. .-. ..- / - ..- -....
..- .... / -.... --- - .-.. ..- / .-. -.... ..- . ...- .-. -... .- --- -- / --- -. / ..- ... .-.
--- ....- - - ..- Always giving parties, to cover the silence. -.- -..
/ - . .... .-. --- -.- -... ... / --.- -... . / --- . -. ..- / .-. --- -.... .-. .- .-. -... ... .
..- -.... ..- -- ..- -... ..- .-. / .--- --- -. .-.-. / *Exit* [Soothsayer]. .- .. -.. ... --- .
.-.. / -. . .... .-. --- . -.... ..- / - ..- / .... .-. ..- .-. --- .... -.... ..- / .... .-.- -- . -.-. ..-
--- -... / .-. ... --- --- . ...- / - .-. -.- .- .... --- --- -.- ....-. -.- .... -... /
--- -.. / - ..- / .-. ..- ..- ..- -... . .-.. ..- -.. / ..- ..- / .-.-. --- -.... .-. -.-. .-. -....
/ --- -.- / .... / .-. .-. --- -.... ... ..- / - ..- / .... --- / -- --- -.... -.... .-. / - ..- / --. ---
-... .-.- --- ... .-.-.- [*To* G—.] ...... / ..- ... ...- / ... . .-. ..- / . --- - -..
.... / ..- .-. --- .-. .-... -.... ..- / -- ..- --- --- ..- .... .-. ..- / .-. ... --- -- ..- -.. .-. ..- / .-.
.. .-. ..- ... ..- / .... .-. -. . .-. .. ..- / *Striking his head.* ... --- . ...- -.
-.... -- --- . / ... .-. --- . .-.. -.... .- / ... .-. --- . ...- -- --.. .-.- -- --- . / ... .-. --- . .
-.... .-. .-. / .-. ... .-. .-. -. --- -.... ... ... --- -... . .-. ... ..- / -.... --- --.-. ..- .-. ..- /
.-. ..- -.. ... .-. -.. / --.- --- -... ..- / ... . --- / -.- .-. -... .- ... / -.-. --- --- ..- .-.-. /
..- ... .-. / .-. --- --- . .-.-. / ... . / ..- --- .-. -.... .- .... / .-. ... -.- ... -- ..- .-. / .- ...
/ ..- ... .-. ..- / .-. -. --- ... ..- .-.-. / .... / .-. .-. --- -- -- ..- -.- .-. .-.- / .-. --- -. --.
-.-. .... .-. -.-. "Another thing that lends me a fine feeling of security
is the opportunity to convey misinformation," she writes. "To
chat on and on and on about 'my life.'" -... . -... . / -.-. --- .-... .-. .-. --- /
-- --- .-. .-. ..- .-. .- ..- . / -... .-. --- ..- / -... ... --- / .-. . ..-. ... .-. --- / -..- -.. .- .. -.-. -... --.
--- -.... ... ..- -.- .-. ..- ..- / .-. .- --- / ... --- . .-. .-. / -... ... / .... .-.- .. -.- .-. --- / -.-
--- -- --- / --- -.-. . ..- .. ..- -.... -- ..- --- -... MMTTITMNATJMMST-

MONIA. ..-. --- -... .-. ..- / .... ..- . -.. ..- / ....- .. ..- / ..... --- / --.. ..- /
....- . -.. ..- -- / .-. .- -.. ..- -.. ..- -.. / ..- . .-.. ..- ... .-. ..- . .-.. / ...- --- -.. /
. -.. -... ..- -... / --- -... .-. ..- .-.. / ..-. ..- -... .... .-. ..- -.. -... - ..- -.. / .....
..- . -.. ..- / --. --- -... ..- -... ..- / --. ..- .... . .-. .-. ..- .-.- / Enter a Servant,
others following.] .-.. -... --- -.. ..- -.. . / . .-.. / - ..- -.. / --- -.. .-. --. ..- -.
.-.-.- / --- -.. .. ..- -... .-. -.- .-. -.. ..- -. / . ...-.. / . .-.. / - ..- -.. / --- -.. .-. ....-.
-..- -. .-. -... ..- -.. -.. .-. .-.-.- / ..- . .-.. / --. ..- .-. -.-. -... --- .-. .-. ..- -.. ..- -... / ..... .-..
. --- -- ..- .-.-.- / -.- --- -- .-. .-. --- .-.. . .-. .. .-. ..- ... / - --- .-.. ..- / --- ... .- ..- -.. / ..-.
-..- -.. .-. -.. .-. ..- . --- -.. ..- ..- .. ..- -.. / ..-. --- -... ...- --- ..- .-. -.. / ....- . .-.. ..- .- ..- -.. / ..- .
.-. ..- ..- ... .-. ..- . ... .-.-.- / Enter [below] B— [in his night-gown] with
Servants and torches. -..- -.. . - / - --- .... / --- ... .- .... / ..-. -.. .-. -... /
-.. . .-. -. .-.. .... .-. .-. / - ..- --- --- -.. / .-... -..- .... -.-. .-.-. / .- --- --- .... / - ..- .-..
/ --. .... --- -.-. --- ... / .-. .-. --- -- -- --- -.. . - / --- --- -.. . - / .-. .-. --- -.. .-.. .-... --- ...
/ ..... -.-- --- .... .-.. .. ..- -- / -..- -- / . .-. -... / --- --- . ..- -... / ..- -.. / - --- --- .... /
..- -... / ..-. .-. -..- -... / ....- / ..... .-.. --- .-. -.- -.. - -- --- ... ..- / .-. ..- .-. . -... ..- -..
It's in the final stages of dysentery that things become interest-
ing as past the last anal gasp the sphincter continues to grasp
as though there were some remaining Salvo to discharge. That
final heave, however, would produce straight away the rectum
itself (an impossible exchange).

But we strain at that threshold, pink ring protruding, in plea-
sure and in pain—to give such carnage birth. -. --- .-. .-. .-. ..- --- -...
/ -.-. -... --- -... .. --- / ..- .... -.-. -.-. ..- -... -.- --- / -. .-. / . ..- / --- -- .-. -...
..- . .-... --- Hierarchies are built on boredom (misinformation)—
I am—and anything "new" is a beginning, anything "old" re-
membering.

Anything new bores—makes a hole in—the old.

But there's no tomorrow without remembering—no dream-
ing—only now. The traction screws groove to turn clockwise
in my head.

Make it now.

Bravo Zulu.

But we remain, like it or not, built of boredom. -..- .-. ..- --- -..
--. / .-. --- -... .-... -... .-.. / .-. .-. --- -... .. .-. .-. .-. ..-.. .-.. / --- .-. .-. / ..... .-.

--- -... -.. ..... / -.. --. / --- -... --- .... .-.-.- / [*Draws a knife.*] --- -.. .. --. /
..- -... -... --- -... / -.. --. / -- --- --- . -- . --. -. .-- .-... ..-.- / .-.. --- --- / . .--.
. -.. --- --. -- --- -- --- ... --- --. . / -.. --. / .--. --- --. -. .-- -- --- -.. .-.-.- /
[*Music plays.*] --- -.. --. / -. . .-... --- .--. / -.. --. / -. . . -.. .-- --- -- --- -. /.
-.-. . --. .-... / --- -... --. / .-. .-- --. -.. --- .- -.. .-... --- ... --- / -.. --. / -- --.
--- / -.-. --- .-.. --- .... .-... / --- -... --. / -.. --- .-- --- ... --- -.. .. --. -.....- --.
--- ... --- -.. --. / -.. --. / --- .-. . ... -.. .. --- / --- .-.. / --- -.. --. / ..... .-.
-..- -... -.. ..... / -.. --- / .-. --- .... -.. .. -.. .-... -.. / -- .. -.. . .-... --- / -.. --.
/ --- ... --- -.. --. -.- --- -.. / .-.. -.- --- .-. --- -- ... / -.- --- --. .-. --- --.
/ ..... . -.-- --- / -- . ..... -- --- / -.- --- -- -. --- .-... --- -.- --- -.. / --- -.. --. /
-.- --- -.. .-... -.- --- -. -.. --. / -.- --- .-. --- -.. -. --. -.- --- --- -.... -. --- --. / -.- .-.
--- -.. --. / --. -.. -.- -- --- --- /-.. --. / ..... --- / -.-. --- --- --. / .-. --- --- --- -- --. .. .-.
--- -.. / -.. --. / . ..... --- -.. --. / -. -.- -.-. -.. --- - / -.-. --- --- -.- . .-.. / -.. --- / --.
-..- ..... .-.. --- / --- -.. --. / -- --. --- --- / .-... .-- --- / .-. --- --- -. .-- --. --- ... .-.. /
..- --- -.. .-.- / -.- .-.. --- --- -.. --. / -.- -- --. --- / -.- --- -.. -.. --- ... / --- .-. . /
/ ..... --- / . ..... --- .... . -- / -.. --. / . ..... --- -.. --. / .-. --- --- -- .--- / -.. --- /
-.-. -.-. -.-. -. --- --- -.- .-.-.- / *Sound a flourish, with drums.* -.. --. -. .-..- -. ... .-..
/ -.. --- / --- -.. --. / .-. --- --- -.. --. -- --- --- -.-. .-. --- / -.. --. / . / ..... --- -.. --. / -.-.
--- --. -- --- .-. / .-. --- --- --. -.- --- --- .-. --- --- .... / -.. --. / -.- --- --- .-.
--- -.- --- --- -.. / --- -.. --. / -.- --- --- -.. --. / -.... -.. - . ...-. --- --- ... .- - / -.-. --- --. ....

--- In me there are ECPs I'll never show—there isn't time—but
we all have them and may, from the top of our heads to our toes,
open our minds.

Moment to moment, what we hold together holds us true. ....
--- .-.. -.-.- / -. / ... ..- -. ..- -... / - .--- -.. / - -..- --- / -. / .-. --- -. --- / --- -
--- After what time we have is gone through there's always some
left unused, unsaid, to gather and dangle out ahead.

Darkness and terror.

The crater's immediately under the monster.

"Be still!".... -..- . .-.. / .-. --- -- -- --- -.. / --- .-.. / --. --- -. . .... .-.-.- / --.
--- . .... / --- .-.. / --. .-- .. . -.. -. . ...- - -.- .-.-. / -.. -.. -.. ... / --- -...
/ -. .-.-- -.. / .-.-- -.. / --- .... -.-. -.. -.. -.. -.. . -. / --- / --- -.. - - / .-- .. - . /
-- -.-.- -.. / .-.-- -.. / -.... -. .-.- / -.-. .. - .... / -.-- -.. / .-. / --. .-- -.-. ...
..- . .- - .... - . --- / -.. --- -.. .-.. -.. -.... .-.-.- / [*Aside.*] --- -- / -.. - -.. -.. -.

-.-- .-- / -.-. .-- .-.. -. / - . .-- .-- ..- - / ..- -..- / ..-. .-- ... / -.-- -.. .-- / - ---- - /
-.-- / .-. -. .-- --- -... --- ..- And then we're going to blow up stuff,
light people on fire. -. --- -... / .... . --. --. .- -... / .... .-. ..- -.. .-- -.. .-.-. /
Enter four or five of the Guard of A—. --. --- -.. .-- --. --- -... / --- ...- /
..- -.. / -.- --- -- .--. / ..-. .--- -... / --- .-.. .-.. / ...- --- -... --- / - ..- -... --- .... /
/ ..-. .-.- -... ....-.. --- -... / ..-. .--- -... -.-. .- -... ..- - / ..-. .--- -... / -. --- --.
.-.. / -.-. .... --- - .-.. -... .-.- .-. .- / --- -... --. -.- ... --- -.- .... / --- .-.. .-.. /
-. .--- / ..- -.. / ..-. .... --- .-.. .-.. --- / --- ...- / - .. --- -- -... ..- -.. / . / --- .-.. /
..- -.. / -- . -... ....-.. -.. --- -... -.. .. --- / . / -. --- -... .-.. / ..-. --- -... / ---
.-.. .-.. / -. .-- .-.. --- / . .-. --- / -- . ...-.. .-.. --- -... / -.- .-. .-.. -... -.- ..... .-..
-... . . -.. --. We glory in simple, sing-along word sets and splash in
waves of hysteria, cooked-up emotions and wild mass partisan
propaganda-fed passions. Observe how the slogans, coded to
some culture fable, crest on the surge to form tension spikes for-
ever predicated on near-term catastrophes, collapses, that bristle
at the edge of the hole (the monitor).

But mingled in Earth's dust is a measure of beauty. It is
that—not lips of clay—we kiss with a hundred ecstasies. .... ..- ..-
.-.. . --- / --- .-. -. / -... . --- / .-. -... --- .-- .-. -... .. .-. .... / -. --- --. -. .-. .- . - ..- -...
/ ...- . .... .-.- ..- -... / -... . -... -- . . --- -... / . / - .. --- -... .-. .-. -. . -... --- .-. .- / --. -...
-.. .-- -- -- --- -... .. / .... --- --. -. .-.-. --- / ..-. -... .... --- --- - / - ..- / .... --- .-. .- -. . ..- . - .-.-
.- / [A— *dies.*] --- .-. -. / - ..- .-.. / .... --- ..-. .-.. .-. .-.. .-.- / .... --- -- / --. --- -...
.... / . / .... -.-- ..-. .-.. ..- / --- .-.. .-.. / ....-.- --- -... ..... .-.- -.- Most of
our lives we've been hooded. By "hooded" picture a prophylactic
as concretely efficacious as the burqas worn in fundamentalist
worship or the black sacks knot over the heads of those detained
within corporate culture. In both cases the function is to make
their wearers more pliant, though noting—and importantly
in terms of understanding degrees of separation—the former
provides eye slits whereas the latter don't. In fact sometimes the
detained have their eyes taped shut in addition to being black-
dropped.

The hood's the con: namely there exists a separation formed
of word pap between how and what we believe we are—our be-

ginnings and ends—and what's happening, going off, around us within which we've unbeknownst COB no sway.

Feet however may be partially free and even hands, and we may gesture a little, even if it's to our own shade.

FTFO. --- - --- -.- ---- -.. / --- -.. .- --- / -- ..- -.. .- ..- -.. .-. .-. --- -... .-.- / .... -..- ---- .-.- --- -. / - .- --- / -.- ..- .-. .--- --- -- ..- / - . .-.- -... --- .... -..- -.. --. / - . -... .-.- .- .-.- -.- ---- / .... ..- -... .-. -.- -.- / - . -... .- .- -.- ---- / ....- -..- .- . - .... . .-.-.- / *Enter* [*from opposite sides*] C— [*with his sword drawn*] *and* C—. --- -.. .-.. .-. -.- / ..- -.. .-. -.- -.- --- -.. / .-.. ..- .- ---- -. / ....- -.-. --- --. -.. ---- . / .... --- ... --- -. / ..... --- .-.. -.- / - --- ... --- -. / .-.-. ..- -.. - .- - -... .-.. -.-. --- .- -.. / ....- -- --.- -.. --- / -.- --- --- -.. -.- / -- ..- -..- - ..- -.. -.. -.-. --- / --- .-.- -.- -.- -.-. / --- .-.- .- / [*Sleeps.*] ....- --- -.. - -.. --- .-. ---- -.. -- / ---- ..- ..- --- --- .-.- / -.-. -.- --- -... -- / .-.- -.. -.. --- .... ---- .- --- -.. / - --- -.. / -- --- --- -.. ..- .- -.. -.. --- .- -... .-.- / -.- ..- -.-. .-.. ..- -.. -.-. --- .... -.- -.. - -.. .- -.- ---- -.. -.. / - . .-. --- --- -.- . ...- / - ..- -.. -.. -.-. --. -.-. --- ..- / -.-. ..- .- -.- -.. . --- -.- ---- -.. / .-.. ..- .- -..- . --- --- / -.- --- --- .... . -. / -.- ..- --- .... ..- .- / ..... --- -- -.- ---- -.. ---- .-. / .... --- -- -- ---- ---- What government will happily permit its subjects to free themselves from its own rhetoric? Just as the show heats up, what theater troupe throw up the lights?

Or draw aside the curtains to reveal an empty stage.

It is then we lose our illusions—what had survived even after the end of hope. - --- -.. . / -.-. ... ..- ..- .... .-.. / --- - --- ... --- -. / -- ..- -... ..- .-. --- INKSBAOPTSTICAMF. ....- / ... .- .... .-.. .-.. ..- -- / - .-.. / .-. .-.- -.-. ..- .-. .-.- --- / .-. .-.- --- -.-. -.- .-.- .-.- ..- / ..- -.-.- / .-. .- .- -.- .-. .- --- / -.. .- -- / .-. ..- .- -.- .-. ..- ---- / - ..- / ..... --- -.- ..- .- ....- .-.-.- / --- -.. / -.-. .-. -.- ..- .-.- ..- ..- . .- --- .-. . / -- --- ---- -... -... ..- ---- / - --- .. .... / --- .. --- ..... / --- .-. ---- ..-. ---- .... / ..- / -... .- --- --- / ..- ..... .-. -.- ..- ..- .-. . - --- .-.- / [*Steps forth.*] -- --- .... / ..... -..- --- / .- ..... -.-. .-. --- .... --- / .- .... ..- -.. ..- .- / - ..- ..- .- ..- / .-. .- --- -.. ..... -.- / -.- .. -.. .-. - .... / ..- .- -.- .- --- --- .... / .- -.- -.- .. -.- --- .--. / --- -.- ..- / .- .-.-. .-.- ..- --- / ..- .... .-. -.. --- / ..... --- -.. .- . - .. / --- / .-. .- --- / ..- ..- .-. / -.. .- -.-. ..- -.. / ..... --- --.- -.. ..- -.. / -.- .- --- / -- / --- / .-. ..- .- -.. ..... --- -- ..- -.- .-. .-. --- / ..- -- / -.- .-.- -.- ..- / ..- .-. -.- .-. - --. ..- / -... ..- -.-. --- -.. .-.. ..- .-.. ..... Let's break this one too, and then they'll be equal. --- .-. . - .-.- / --- .-.- .-. .-.- ... / -.-. -.- --- / .-- -.-. -.-. / --. -. --- ... / -.- -.- .... --- -.. / .-.- -.- / -.- / ..- --- --- --. -. . - --- / --. -. -. --- ... / ..... .-. -.- .-. -.-. ..- ..- -.- --- / ... --- -. . --- -- / -... / .- -.. --- ... .- Like a spider quiet and motionless I can

sometimes hear the brainwash—purr of computer god containment policy. On more than one occasion this has saved my life.
- --- .... / .... ..- -.-. ..- -.. / ....- . ..- .... ..- -.. / -. .--- -.. --. .-.. / -..- -.. - / -...
-..- -. .-.. .-.-. / - . ..- / ....- .--- -.. / -- .--- .--- .-. ..- .... .-.. .--- .-.. / .--- -.-. ..-.
-. .--- -... ..- -.. / - . ..- .... ..- / -.. . .-. -. .-.. / .--- ....- . -.. / .... .--- -.. -
..- -.. -.. / .--- ... . / ..- . .-. ..- / .... -.-. .-. -.- ..- / .-. .-. .-. .-.. / --.. . ..- -.
..- -.. / .-- --- .... / -.. -- / . .-. -.. / -- . .-. .... .-.-.- / Enter the Prince [and
Attendants]. ..- .... / . .... .-. . / ..- . .-. / -... --- - / -- --- -.. .-. . ..- -...
.-.. / -- --- ....-. / .-. . .- .... .-. ..- / --- -.- . ..-. / - ..- -- / -- . .-. .-. .-.
..- .... / - ..- .... / -. .--- -.-. . -. .... -.... ..- -.For all the emphasis on mission asymmetry, however, we retain in general the idea of theft.
That's why we lock on a missing part.

Or fear equals the unintended: It hugs, holds in state, what we want in what we don't, where what we need is here scrambling to render a—what?—pang.

Sic. Sic. Sic. Sic.

FIGMO. -. --- / - -..- ... .- .... .-.-.- / --- -.. / - --- / .-. -. .--- . .-...
- ..- / ..- . -.. ..- .--- -.-. .-. -. .-.. / .... ..- .--- .-.. / -... .--- . .-.. -.. .-.. / -. .--- .-. -.-. -.
--- . -... / -.-. -. -.... ..- . ...- .-.-.- / [Aside to her sons.] -. .--- ... - ..- --
--- -.. / -.-. ..- -.. -.. -.. ..- .-.-.- / . / .... / -- .--- - -.. ..- .... / -- .--- -...
.-.-. -. --- - -. / --- --. -.-. .... / --- .... / --- / .-. .... --- ....- .-.. / -- .-. --- .-..
-. .--- .-.. / .... / .... .--- / - -.. --- --. --. --. ..- - / . .--- ..- .-.-.- / [Kisses
T—.] ... ..- / ....- --- - -. / -.. --- / -.. .- ..- --- -.. .-.- / .... --- -. .-. -.
--- . -. .-.. / --- -- -- --- .-. -. / --- --. -.-. .... / -. .-. ..- . -.. / --- -.. / --- -.. /
--. .-. --- -- -. .... --- .-. . .-.. / . .... .-. ..- .-. . -. / --- -.. / .-. ..- .... ..- . .-..
..- . .... .-.-.- / Clock strikes. .... ..- --- / .-. -. -.. --- .-. -.-. / -- ..- / .... ..- --- .-...
/ -. .--- .... .-.. .-.. ..- Emotion and beauty equal the body thinking and the mind touching.

Reason nests in awe.

The rest is treason. .-. --- -- ..- / - -..- ... .- .... / --. ... --- --- .-. -.
/ --- -... --- . -.. -.. / --- -.. / --. .-. --- . ...- / .--- . ...- .... .-.. / --- --.
-..- .... / . -.. . .... / -- ..- --- . ..- / -.. --- -.-. --- .-. -. / .-. -.. -. .-. -- / .-.
--- - / --- .-. --- / .... ..- / - ..- --- -.. --- .-. --- -. / --- -. -. -.. .... / .-. ..- / --- /
-.-. -. ..- .-. .-. -. / -.. --- ... .-. --- -. .-. -. / .-. .... --- -.. / ..- . ..- / --- / -.-. .-. ..- .

.-.. -. / The death's head's lodged in the upper right, which we can visualize only via a "dancing eye" pattern mimicking those unconscious flicks or micro-saccades long considered mere motor noise though actually actively controlled by the same spasm that hugs what eyes scan these lines.

And here it comes UYA. --- -... --- / .... . --- / .-. -. ..- / .... . / .-..
-... --- .-.. .-.. . / --- -.-. .... . --- / -.-. ..- .... .-.. .--- ... .-.. / --- / --.- -..- --- ...
.-. -. ..- / ...- . ...- / .... .-. -... -.-. .-.. .--- ... --- / - . / .-. ..- -.. ..... --- -...
..- / .-.. -... --- .-. .-. .--- / .-. -... ..- .-. . ..... --- -- ..- -.. .-.. ... / ..... -.. ...
... --- / -- --- -... .. ..-. ..- ..... .-. .--- --.. . --- -.. ..- .-.-. / [Kneeling.] -..- -..
/ .-.-. ..- -.. .... . .--- -... --- / .-. -. ..- / -. --- / ..-. --- .-. .-. .-. --- / --- / .-.
..- --.. --.. . It wasn't the men but their smell she brought home—a scent no amount of showering seemed to absorb. Or it was more than a smell maybe, as though their cries were soaked into her skin that, translucent, one could see through into the pit. -- --- /
-..- -.. --- / .-. -. --- -... .-.. ..- / - .- .... --- / .... --- --. --. .. --.. --.. --- /
..- / -- --- . / ....- / .-.. -... --- ..- / .-. --- --- -.. .-. . .-.-. / . --- / -.. --- --..
/ .... --- / .-. .-. ..- -... .-. -. ..- / . . --- / .... --- / - . / - . .-.. ..- / -. .-. ..-
..- .... .-. ..- --- / .-. --- --- .... --- / ..- / .-. ...- --- -.. ..- / . .... / ....-. -.- .-.-. /
Knock within. -. --- / .-. --- -..- .... --- / ..- / ...- --- ... --- -.. .-.. --- /
..- / ..-. --- -.. .-. --- / ..- / -- .- -.. --. --.. . / .-. ..- -.. / ..-. --- -.. ... ... --- It
is desirable to have those people wittingly or not, red on red, falter first, but we mustn't wait until in some perfect bat-turn conditions lock. Rather bring them on—hurl with all our might against anything CenComm. ..- .... ..- -- .-.. . / .-. ..- ..- -.. -... --- / ...
--- -... .- --- / ..- .... --- -.. .-. ..- --- -.. ..- / -- ..- .-.-. / Knock. .-. ..- .... .-..
. .- --- -.. .. ..- / -.- .-. ..- ..- .... .-. ... --- / ..- .... ..- .-.. .-. --- / - . / -- --- .-..
.... --- / ..- / ... --- / .-. .- --- -... .. .-. --- / / .... --- / .-. -.. .- . / -.. .-. . . --- .-..
--- / - --- / -..- -... / .-. -.. .-. ..- .-. .- --- ..- / - ..- .. .-. --- .-. .-. --- / ..- / .-. --- ..-
-.. .. --- -... --- An operative is held "by both hope and fear" the early modern allegorist (not woodcutter) wrote, though a tree mirrors the lungs' structure albeit attached to the photosynthetic "breath" (the "harness") of Earth through which its roots wend.

Moreover they say the man in the moon's a wood-stealer who

having committed a trespass was transported there as punishment. He may be seen there today with the axe on his back and in his hand the brushwood bundle.

Plainly enough the water-pole of the heathen story has been transformed into the axe's shaft, the carried pail into the thorn brush.

He's the one who goes naked to the center of the maze to slaughter the bull-headed monster of the double axe, the labris from which we derive "labyrinth." ... --- / .-. --- .--. ..- / . -.. ...- . .... . -.-. . ...-.. ..- / ..- .... .-.. / -- . -.. .-. .-. ..-/ [*Seeing the body.*] -- --- .-.. .... --- .-.. .-.. --- / ...- --- -... .--- ..- / --- -.. .... -.- .-.. -.. . .-.. --. / ..... --- -- / .... -.- --- ..- - ..- / -.. --- -... / -. .-- -.. / . -.. .-.. ..- / -.- --- -.. / -. .--- ... ... --- .... / .-.. ... ... -.-. --- -.- --- .-.-.- I sense our choice is facing either a mirror or a monitor. --- .-. -. / -.. --- -... / -. .--- -.. / .-.. --- ... --- -... / - ..- .-.. / --- -... / - ..- -.. / ...- --- - / .-. . .-.. -.. -.. .... / . / . / -. .--- -.. ..... / -. .--- --- -... .-.. ..... --- I have been a water molecule in the sky and the tooth of a dragon.

I have been a tree at the edge of a volcano, a hundred hands. ...- --- -.. -.. ..- -... / -.- --- -.. / .--- --- -- / . -.. .-.. ..- / ...- --- -.. .-. ..- --- / .-. .--- / - ..- -... --- .... / -.-. ..- -.. --- -... .-.-.- / [*They whisper.*] - ..- -.. / -... --- -.. ... . / .. -. --- / -... --- -.. .-. / - --- .-. .-. .-. --- -.. ..- / -- --- -.. -. . --- / .... --- .-. .-. ..- -... / - .-- -.. / --- -.. .... ..- -... / -. . -. / ..... --- -- / .--- --- -- -. / . -.. .-. .-. ..- / .-. .... --- -.. .-. .-. --- -... ..- / --- .-. -. Taking out the garbage. .-. -. -.. --- .-. --- -.. -.. .-. -. . --- / -. .-. --- / ....- . / -- .-.-.- --- / -- .-. --- ... .-. --- / --- -. / -.- . / .-. ... --- .-. .... .-. -.. / --- / -- .-. -. .-. -. -. -. -. .-. / --- -. .- / -.-. -.. --- --- -. -.- / . -. --- ..- / -. -.-. -. ... --- --- --. -.- / - . --- ... .-. --- ... On every bill and coin is a mugshot of a president—and so on all our money is a reminder of our debt to crime (society). Money of course is debt and it's edged in pain given and taken: a constancy, a threshold.

There is no mugshot of the bloodied. ..- ... / .-. .. ..- .- -.. -.. . .... / ... .- --- / ....- -... / -.-. -.. .-. --- / .- .... .- .-. .-. . --- / -.. --- .-. .-.. -.-. -.. --- ... / .-. . --- -- / -.. -.. -.. / -- --- -... .-. . .-. . / --- -- -.-. / .-. .. ..- -.-. -.. .-. . .... --- ... / . / . / -.. -.. -.. . --- / ..-. ..- .-. -.. -.. -.-. --- - .- -... The world burbling ungroans on, power's jaws open, always ready to deflower—to strip, arms outstretched, from under the wreckage of a past civilization the thought-to-speech-to-text mojo. . --.- --- .--- / ..- / .-.. ..- / .-. .... .-.. / .-. -.-. -... .... / ..-. -.-. -... -.-. -- --- / ..- / -.-. -.. ..- / ..- / -... -... -... .. .--- / ..- / -.- .. --.- ..- / ..... . / ..- -... ..- / ..-. .. -... .... / -.- --- ... -.-. -.-. -... / .-.. ..- / .-. . ...-.. / -.-. -.. ..- / ..- / - --- / .-. .-. -.- .--. / ..... . / -.- --- ... .-. .... -. ..- .-.. / ..- / .... -... --- -... --- / ..- / ...- - .. -.-. .-.. -... / .-.. ..- / -... .--- ..- -... -... .-.. .. -... ---.. ... ..- / --.- ..- / - --- / .-. .. ..- / -.-. -. .-. -.-. .-. -... / ..- / --- .--- -... .. .-. / -.-. . .-- / -.-. -.. -.-. -... ..-. . . - The out-of-focus moments. One after another after the next.

Mistake after mistake after mistake. .-. --- ... / -.. --- .-.. . .-. . --- / ..- -.. / -.-. .. -.. .. ..- -... --- ... / .-.. ....-. .-.. -... .. .-. / --- .-. -.-. -... --- -.-. --- - --- / .-. -. --- ... --- / ..... -.- --- / .... . -... -.. -.- --- -.-.- / [Friar stoops and looks on the blood and weapons.] ..- -..- / .-. .. ..- -.. --- / -.-. -.. .. -. --- / -.. --- .-. .. -.- / - .. / ----- - / .-.-. --- -... --- / --- .-. -... --- .-. -. --- ... --- / --- Í / ..-. --- -... / --- The polite, delicate and decent are different names for hypocrite, liar and coward. Nor's there a difference between what we think and what we do—for to think's to do.

But that doesn't portend we want to blow out our brains to Foxtrot our own skulls.

Or do do but we ought to think before we do. Give thought to where we do and what's there in what we do—and when and how—what position we assume and how others are around us— their arrangement and timing. ..- -.. .-. --- -.. .-.. .-.. -... ..- / --- / -... ..- .... .-. -.-. --- .... .-. -... --- / ..- -.. .-. -... --- ..- / --- .... / .-. . ...-. .. --- .... / - ..- / .-. -.-. --- ... --- ...- -... --- .... / .-. .- ...- .-. -.- ..- The vine grows spirally up its prop portending resurrection.

A house appears. A bed in a room. A complex of tensions, all of which, sexual in origin, occur inside our heads.

Its movements mimic the dance of the cock performed for a hen audience quacking with excitement. The cock flutters in circles with a hobbling gait, one heel held ready to strike a rival's head. ..- -.. .-. --- -.. .-.. .-.. ..- / --- / -.... ..- ..... .-. --- .... .-.. ..- -.. -. .-.. -.... ..- / --- .... / .-. -.. . ...-. -.-. --- .... / ..- / .-. -. --- ... --- .... ..- / --- / .-. -.. -.-. --- .-.

-..- --.. --- - --- .... / .-.. -. .-- "Living with what I know has become a horror, like a red halo—a red circle with bright matter in the middle of it—and that I can be discovered," she writes. . ...- -- / -. -..- .-- --- / .--. -. . .... -.-. -.-. / .... / -. .--- .-.. -. / .--- .... . -... / -.-. . ..-- .- / -..- .-.. -. -. .. / -.-. / --. -. .--- ... / -.-. -.-. ... ... / - -.-. -.. --- -- . .-. .... / --. ..- -.. ..- -.... --- ... . / .-.. .--- --- -.... .-.. . -.-. --- ... --- -... -- .. -.. -.. . .-.. / . .-- ..- --. --. -. --- -- -. -.-. ..-. -.... .-.. .-.. . .--. -.. .-.. --- --- / -..- / ... / . .-.. -..- --- -.-. .--- . ..- .-.. / -. ..- -- --Someone had painted an X visible in the sunlight near the shadows cast by the trees. This does not mark the correct spot, but it's become part of the area's lore and so is maintained. .--- --- - . / -.-. . .-.. .. --- / --- -- --- .-.. / -..- .... --- -. . --- / -..- -.. -. . .-. .-. -.-. / -- .-- -. -.. ... .. --. -. -. -.-. -.-. . -... -.. -. . -. -.-. --- -. .. / -.-. .-. .-.. .. -. -.... --- -. -. / -.-. . ...-. --- ... --- --. . . I am the four crows on the phone line outside the kitchen window—eight eyes ready to play servant to paranoiac trances in which time's suspended in spiritual spasms indistinguishable from the ineffably beautiful moment that precedes an epileptic fit. -..- -. / ..- . .-- .-- .-- / -.-. .-- .... .-- -... / -.. --- . -... / .. .-- .... .-.. / .-.. -.-. .-. .-. .-. .- -.-. -.. / ... --- .-. .-.. ... .. / -.-. -..- .. . . / -.-. -.-. ... --- -. .-. -. Actually it is really quite simple: With vigilance, cunning and pluck a player can maintain a sense of orientation in space and ponder paradoxical subtleties within a dangerous sinuous maze. .-. .. -.... ..... -.-. -.. -. .. -.. -.... ..- / -. -.-- --- -.. / .- -.-. -.-. .. / --. -.-. --- -.... .. / - ..- .-. / .-. -.-. / .. -.-. --- -.. / -- ..- - .... . .- ..- -.. -.-. .-. . .-. [Falls.] - .. / -- ..- -. ..- -.. ..- .... -.-. ..- -.. / .-. -.-. --- -.. ... ..- -.. .-. --- -. .. ..- // / -- ..- -. .-. --- --- ... . -..- / ..- / .-. -.-. --- -.. / -. --- -.. -- / .... --- -- / ..- -.. / .-.. ..- --- / -. -.-. -. -. . .-. -..- -..- / -. .-. .-. . .... / -.. -.. / -. .--- ... --- -. / --- .-. -. / ... .-- . -. - .. / .... -.. -. .... / .--. --- ..- --. / .- -- -.. -. / .... . -.. .-. -.-. / -- -.-. . --- -.. / .-. -. .-. ... -.-. -... -.-. .- ..- -.- / --. -. -.-. ... . -.-. -- --- -.. ... / -. ..- . .-. ... -.. / -. . --- --- The information we give up—as individuals and as a pack—is consummately harvested to manipulate us. We are reaped like wheat—scythes level to the right, to run the blade across the eyes.

The use of questions and answers.

The old life's buried, and a new and different being begins to appear. ..- ... ...- -... / .... --- -- / ..- -.. / --. .--- ... --- -. .-. / -. .-- .... .-..

/ ..-. --- ... .-.. / . / ..-. .--- --- .-.. .... .-.. ..- / -.... --- -.. --. / .... ..- / - ..- -... / ..-. .--- -..- / ..-. .--- -.... .-.. .--- --- -..- / .-..... / .--- .-.. .-.. ..- -.. .... .-.. ..- / -.-. --- -.- -.-. ..- / --- ..- .-.. .-.. ..- / -.... --- -.. .-..... / --- --.. / ...- .-.. -.... --- --- --- .-. ..-. / .-.. --- / -. ... .---- --- / - ..- / --. .-.. --- --- -... / . / - --- --. ...- -... / [A bell rung.] .... ..- ... ..- / --- --- / - .-.. --- .-.. ..- / .- -.. .-. .-. / - .-. / . / ..-. --- -... .-.. .-. . ..- -.. / --- ..- ..- .-.. ..- -.... .-. --- ..- / - . .-. ... .-.- / [Thunder and lightning.] ..-. --- -... / .-. .. . .- ..- -.. / .- --.. / ..... --- --- / .. .--- --- .... .-.. ..- / .- --- ... -. -. -- -. / ..- .--- .- -.. .-. / ..... --- --- / ... .-. .-. .-. / -.... .... .-. .- -.. / --- .... ..- .- -. .--- ..- - ...-. / -.-. --- .- ..... .-.. / . / -. .-.. --- -.. .- ..- -.. / --- --. / -- ..- - / --- -.... -- .- -.. ..- / -.- .-. .... ..-. .-. -.... --- -.- .-. ...- / ..... --- --- / -. --- -.. / ...- ... .- / -.. --- ...- -.. / - .-.. ...

There is blood on all money—money in our purse or vest pocket. In our money clip or wallet. The blood of children. Egyptian blood. The blood of Goya. Memory.

Shut up and color. .--. ..- - . - . .-- .-.. -. / --- / .... .-.- -..- -.. .-..- / -.-- -.. --- / -.-. .-.-- - - / .-.-- / -- --- .-- .-... / --- -... / - .-.-- -.. . / . / --. .-.-- - / -.-.- -... / -.-. --- .-. -.. .-.. .-. .-. - / --- / -. .- .-- .-- .... .- -.- .-. .-. / .-. --- .- -. -.- --- --- -... - .-..- I am a wind of the sea for depth and a wave of the sea for weight—its sound without breadth.

I am an ox of seven fights and stag of seven tines, a griffon or hawk on a cliff. A tear of the sun among flowers a boar suns himself upon.

I am a hill of words forms, a battle spear poking fire for a head. ..- -... / -.-. --- - / -.-- / .-. .--. .- .-.. -. . --- -..- / -. -.-- -.. / -.-- -... / --- - - --- ... ..- .-. / .... -.- --- - -..- / -.-- -.. / .-. .-. -.. / -.-- .-. -.. -.-.. ... ... - - --- -.. / -.-- -.. / ..... .-.-- .-- .-.- - / -... .-. --- .-.. -.- . - .-.- - / -.. --- -. / . .-- / ..-. .-- --- -.. --- .-.- -.- .-. - - -.-.- / Enter P— with his Page [with flowers and sweet water and a torch.] -.-- -.. / .... .-.-- - - -.-- -.. / -... --- .-- - - / .-. .-.. .-... / .-- - -.. .- -.- - / . / . .-.. . . -.-.- / --- .-. / .- .-.. -.-. --- / -- --- .- -.- .-. .-.-- / --- .-. / .- -.- ..- --- / -- --- -.. .- -.. / -.-. --- ..... . -.-. .... / .- .-.. .- --- .-. -.-.- / / -... --- - / .- . ..... / .--- --- -.- / .... . -.-. .-.- --- -.. ..... / - -.-- / -.-. .-.- .-- -.-- . --- -.-. - / .- -.- / -. .- -.-. -.. --- . .--- / . -.- .-.-- -.. / -.-- -.. / - - .-- / -.-. --. .-.-- -.- / --- -.-.- ..- ... . "It's not too much to say when the word 'blood' is evoked this is a sign reason's about to fart," she writes. ...- --- -..-

.... / --- .... .- .. --.. / ..- -.. .-.. .-.. . -.. / --- / . -- . .-.. .- -.. .. -... / .... --- / -- --- -..
. ..- -... ..- / - --- -.. .-.. / ..- ... ...- / --- .-.. .-.. .- .-. .-.. .. / -. --- -.. -..
..- -.. -. -.. / - .- .... / - . .- .-. .- ..- / - -.-. / .-.. --- -.. -.. .- -.. -.. ..- / -. -. -.. /
--- .-. .-. ..- / .-.- / .... --- / --. --- -- --- ..- / .--- --- --. ..- ..... / - ..- / .... --- .
-... / - ..- / - .- .-. .-. . -.. .- -.. / ..- --- .-. -.. ..- / . -- .-. -.- ... .--- -..
/ ..- .-. / .... ..- / .... --- -.. .-. .-. -.. ..- / --- .- .-. / -.. .. ..- / .-. --- .... /
..- -.. .-. -.- --- --- ..- / .-. -... --- --- .-. / .-.. .-.. --- -.. / .-. --- .-. -.. / ..- -.. .-. .-..
-.. - -... ..- / / -.. .- -.. / .-. -. .- ..- ... ..- .-.- / [*Aside.*] .--- / --- . / ...- -.- / .-.
--- What I mean is WTF does this say, its shoring and clamor up
the shingles toward the swing-slung tree and competitive tow-in
swaying to the rhythm of the heat pattern or syncing of cochlea
to bird cries or traffic words come—and this is what it occurs to
me words come to—to cries—to, among squeals, get from one
place to another—knowing we have—or tried—on the grid.
And to stop death. What the book is. To pump wayang. -. --- .-..
. -- --- -.-. ..- / -- --- ... --- ... --- -- . .-. --- / .-.- --- / .- ..- -.. -. .-. .-.. /
--- .... . .-. -.- -.. .- --- / .... --- . .-.. / .-. .- .-. -.. --- / .-. .-. .- .- .- -.-. --- /
-..- / .- --- / -- --- .- -. ..- .- / .-. --- --- --- / .- .-. -.-. .-. .. .- --- / .-. .- --- -..
..- / ... --- / - --- .- -.. / .-. .- .-. --- / --- .- .-. .... / .- --- --- / -.. .- .... . .-.. --.. .
/ .- ..- .- .-. -.-. / -.. . / .... --- --.. . .- --- / ..... . / .- --- -.. .-. -. .-. --- -.-. --- /
--..- --- . - / .- .-. --- / .- .- .-. .... --- .- -- . / -.. . / .- .-. .-. .-. .- --- --- / -.. .- --- .- --I
have no home in this world anymore. ..- --.. . .-.. / ---- / -. --- -... .--.
..- ... --- / .-. .-. --- . .-. .- .- --- . / .- .. .- ..- .- .... . .-. --- / .-. .- .-. .- / -. .- ..- -.
--- -... / -. .- --- -... / .-. .- ..- .. ... / .- ..- --.. .- --- -... .... / .- --- -. --.. .-. --- ...
--- / --..- .-. -.-. -.. ..- / -. .- .-. --- .... / .- ..- .. --- ..- -.. -. --- -.. .- .- --- /
-. -.. --- .-. ... .- --- -. .. .- .- / [*Reads the*] letter. ..- --.. / . ---- --. .-. / -- ..-
--- -. ..- ..- ... .- .. / .- ..- .- .- . .- .- .. .- -.-. --- / --. .- .- -.. ..- / . ---- .- .- -. . .
/ . --- .- / .- .-. . .- .-. -. .- .. .- -.-. --- / -. .-. .- --- ..- / .- --- -.- .- .- .-. .- --..
..- .-. ..- / ..- - --- --- / ..- -- .. .-. .-. .- .- .-. --- / -. .- .- .- -. .. .- .- --- ...
... / - ..- .- .-. .- .- -. .- -- . --- .-. .-. .- .- .- -. .- / . --- --- / -- --- -.- -.- --- --.. .- .- .- /
..- --.. .- .-. --- / ..- --.. .- .- -.. / .- --- -. .- --- ... .- / -. .- --- -.-. .. .. ..--We rented
a series of railroad flops—a hatch on one end and a corridor.
God knows we are just passing through, an engine out ahead,
though way ahead—a moment distant and hemmed by cliffs. ....

.-. --- .-.. .-. / ...- --- -.. / - .-- / --- -.- .--- .-- / -.... .-- .-. .-. ... . / - ..- /
-.-. .. .- .-- --- -... .-. .-. --. / ...- --- -.. / - .-- / --- .-. .-. .-. ... -. .-. / .-- --- .- -.. /
--- -- / - --- .-. .-. / -. . .-- / .. .- .-. ... / ...- --- -.. / - --- .-. ... .-.- / [*They*
play, and enter the] Clown. ...- --- -.. / - ..- / --. -.-. ..- .-. .-. .- / - .
..- / - --- --. / .-.. ..- / -. --- .- .-. - .- -.. / . ... / .-- --- .- .-.. --- -- / - ..- / .-.
--- -... .- ..- / ... ..- .- ..- .- -.. / - --- .-. / -. . .- / -. ...- .- / .-- --- .- -.. - /
. ... / .- ... .- / .-- --- .- -.. - . .- -.. / --. .- -. -. -. --- .- -.. - . .- -.. / .-. -. --- -.. .- .. I

had a dream: find a woman and place my gun in her. Cleave full-
est practically to the brief bristling pauses in which the rungs go
into each other. ....- / .-.. -... --- .-. .- --- / - ..- / .-. -.- -.- -- .-. .- . -.. /
.... ..- / .-. .- -.. .-. ... --- / --.- .-. .- / --- ... --. .-. .- -. .- --- ... / - ..- / ... --- /
... .- -. -.- .-. .-. --- -.. .-. ... / .-. .- / .- .- ... / --- -.. .-. .- ... .- .-.. --- -. / -... ---
-- --- -. .- --- ... The rich accumulate money to protect them from
its result. I.e. the poor. I.e. fear. I.e. iiee-alalah the mouse ran up
the clock and, jammed in its works, stops. It stops. Blood spurt
over faces. --.- -.-. ..- / .-.. -.- / .- ... .-.- . -.. .- .- -.- / .- -.- ... .- ... --- .-. ...
..- / ..- ... / ..... .- -.. --- / - .- ... / .-. ... .- ... -.-. .-- --- .- -. / .-.- --- -... / .- ...
/ ...- . .- -.- .- --- / ..-. .- --- -- --- / ... --- ... . / ..- --- --- -.- --- --- .- ...
/ - ..- / ... --- / --- -.. .-. ... . .- -.- .-. .- . -- --- / -.. / ..- ... / .-. .- -.- -. .-. .
-- . ..- .- -. .- .- -.- .- . --- / - ..- / .- .- -.- ..- --- / .-.. .-.. ... .- -.- .-.- / ..- ... /
.-. -. .- . .- . ... .- ... --- / --- .- .-.- .- / .- .- --- -.- .- .- / .- .- --- .-.- / -- .- -.- ..- /
-.-. .- .-.. ..... .- --- --.- .- . / *Enter* Murtherers. ..- ... / ... - .- .--- .- --- /
.-.- / ..... -.- / .-.- ..- --- / .- .- ... .-. .- --- .- .- / --- .- .- .-.-. .- --- / --- /
-- .- -.- .- ... / ... --- .... / --- -- ..- .- -.-. .- .- .-. -- .- --- / .-. .-. -.- --- --- .-- ---
--- -.. / --- / ... --- / .- / -... ... .- . .- --- / -.- .- --- -- -. ... .- -. .-.- / .- .- .- ---
.-. .. --- / .--. -. --- -.. / ..- .- --- ...- --- -...To say "no" is the beginning of
conscience, and deniability character as character is destiny or
jouissance juice.

One end in the sun the other in the event.

Anyway it goes on, moonlit, like this.

COTDA. .-. --- / ..- . / --- ... ..- / .- -. -.. .-. --- -- / -- --- -.. ..- / ....
..- ... --. -. .-.. --- --- --- --. -.- .-.- / -.- -.- . / ..... --- .- .-. --- ... --- .- .- / ..- .- ... ...
-... Civilization as we know it has the scent of a terminal illness,
and in turn we each move to the hole in the wall—a glory hole

patriotic bunting is arranged around.

Some face forward, some back, according to the law. -.. . .-.. --..
..- / --- ... .-.- --- .- / .-.. --- . .-- .. / -.. ... . .-.. / .-.- --- . .-.- .-.- --- / -.-.- ... .-..
..- .-.-.- / *Enter* O— [*distracted, with her hair down, playing on a*
lute]. -... --- -. .-.- .. --- / ... .--. .-. .-. --- .- / -- .- . .-.. .- --- / .-.. --- .-.- -.. .-.. ---
/ ... .- .-.- .... / .-.- --- ... .- ... -.. .-.-.- / .--- --- ... .-.- -.- / -. .- --- .-- .-.- .-.- .
-.. .... / .-.. .- .- .-.- . / --- -... --- .- .-.- .-.- .- ... . / .... --- . --- -.. / .--- --- --- ...
... .- / --- -... --- --- / .-.. .- .-.. .-.. .-. .-. / .-- --- .-.- -. .... --- / .... --- .-.. .- .- ..
.... --- .-.-.- Each knows best for him or herself what silence and
nostalgia blooms behind every mask. -.. --- / -.. .-.- .- .-- --- .-.- --- / -..
--. / .-.- --- -.. . .... --- -.. .-. / --- --. --- / .... .-.- .... --- / --- .-.. / .-.. .- --- .-.
--- .- .... / .- --- --- .... / -- --- .-.- .-.- --- .- .... / .-.- --- .-.- .... --- / .... --- / ... .. .
--- -.. .. .- .... / -.. .-- / ... --- -. .-.- .-.. / .... --- -. .... .- / .... --- -. . - / .... --- -.-. / -.. .- --- /
--- -.. .-. / .-.- --- .- -.. .-.- --- --- .-.. / --- .-. .- / --- .- .-. / --- .-.- --- -..
--. .-.-- --- -.. .-.. . .- .-.- .-.. / -.. .- .- / -- .-.- -.. .- --- / --- .- .-.. / --- .-.. --.. / -- --.
--- / -.-. .- --- ....- --- .... / --- --- .-.. / .-.-.- --- .- / .-.. .- .- .-.- --- -.-.- / --- --- -.. --- .-.-. / -- --.
--- -... / -.-. --- .- --- -.. / .-.- .- --- .... / .-.- .- .- / --- .- -. --- -.. .- .- / --- -.. .- --.
-.. .-- / .-- .- .-. .- .- .-.- .- -.-. .... .-.-. .-.. / --- / .... --- / -. .- --- / --- -. --- .-.- --- .- .-.
--- -.. / -.. .- .- -.-. / .-.-. --- -.-.- -- --- / --- .-.- .... / -- --- --- . / .... .- --- / .-.- --- /
-.. --- Human beings are the holes in this planet, and if we leave,
if even for a moment, our bodies unattended they will be towed,
like proverbial ships to nowhere. . --- -.-. .... / -- --- --- -- .-.- / .-- . / -...
-.- .- .- .-.. -.. / --- -.-.- / --- .-.- . / ... .- - . .-.- .-.- .-.. .- .... / .-.- .-.- --- .-.- -.-. / ---
/ -- --- --- --.. .-.- -.-.- / .... --- .-.- .- --- .-.- .-.-.- / When will we elect a president
who was an advertising executive? - ..- -.-.. / --.. .-.. --- --- / -.-. .- --- -.. /
-.. .- -.. .- --- --- .- .- -.. .-. -.. .- -.. .... .-. / ... .- .-.- .-.. .-- --- .-. .- -.. .- / --- -..- .... .-.. -.. .- .- .
.- .-. -.. .-- .- - / -.- .-. .-. .-.- -.-. / .-.. .-.. / .... .-. -.. .- .- -.. .- -.. / --- -.. .-.- .- .-.- .-.-. / -.
..- / .... .-.. .- .- -.. .-.. .- -.. / -.- .-.. / -. .- . --- -.. .- .... .-. / .- .- -.- / --- .-. .-. .-.
..- .- -.. / --- -.- .- -.. .- / - . .- .- .... .- / .- .- .- . .- .- .-.. / -.- .- -.. / - .- -.. / --- -..- .-.
/ - .- .- .... / -- -.. .- .- -.. .-. .- -.. .- .- -- .... / .-- -- .- -.. / - .- .- -.. / .-. -.. .- . .- --- ...
. .-. .- --- .- .-.- / -.- . .-.. .- .- .- -.. .- .- .- .- .-.- - .- .-.. / . .- .. .- .... .- .- .- ....
--- --- .-.. .- .-. / -.- . -.- .-.. .... .-.-. / .-. .- .- --- .-. --- .-. --- .- .- . .- .- --- .-.. --- .- /
. .... .-. .-.- / --. .- .- . .-. .- .-. / --. -.. .- .- .... / -. .-.. .- . .- - .- .- .- .-. / --- .-. .- .-. . .
.- .-. / - --- --- -.. --- .-.- / --. .-.. .- .- -.-.- / --.. .-- -.- .- .- .-. .-. .-.- .-. / [*Stabbing him.*] --- ...

... ..- .... / .-- --- .... / -.... ..- -.- -. -.. .... / ...- --- -.. / - ..- -.. / -.-. ..- .... / .-.. ..- ... . -.-. -. -.. .... / --- -.-. .... / .- .. .. -. .... ..- -- / --. -.-. -.-. -.. - / . .... .-. .. / - ..- -... / .-.. / -.-. ..- .... / .... --- -.. ..- .. / - ..- -... / .-.. ... . / -... .... -. -.-. .. . -. -. ..- -.. / -.. .-. ..- -.-. . -. -.-. / ..- -.. - / ....- .... / . .-. -.. / .... .-.. ..- -. .. ..- -.. / .... ..- .-. -.- -.. ..- -.. / -.-. -. -.-. .-.. ..- -... / - ..- -.. . --- -.. .- ..- -.. .... / .-. -.-. -.-. --. ..- -.. .... / -. -.. ... . --. .. .. .-. ..- -. ...- After killing I keep trembling. I can't eat or talk.

I keep imagining the person begging not to be killed. -.. -..- ... ... --- / ..-. .-. ..- .... .-.-. / .... ..- - / .-. -.. .-. -.-. -.- ... --- -.. .... / --- ... . -- / .--- --- -- ..- .... / --- ... -.-. ..- -... .-. / . ... ..- . .-. .-.. --- -.. .-. --- / -.... ..- -. -.- / ... --- / .... -. -.-. ..- .... -. -. -. -.. / . -. .... - .-.. --- -.-. -- / -- .-. .. . . / .- ..- -.-. .-.. ..- / -.... .-. -.-. -.-. .- - / .-.. --- -.... -. .... ..- -- / ... ..- .. ..- / .-.. -.. ... .--- / -.. / .-.. .-.. --- --- / -. -. -.. ..- .... / --. .-. ... .- ... --- ..- / . -. -... .. .. -.. ..- -- / -. -.. ... -.- .-. ..- -- / ..... .-. ... -... ..- .... / --- -. ... .-. . ...- / . .-. ..-. . -. --- / -. .-. -.. -... --- .-. ..- -- / .-. -.-. -... -.-. / - ..- -... . / .- .-. -. ..-. . / -... ..- -. -. . / -. -.. ..- --- ... .- .... / -.-. ..- .-. ..- / -.. . .... -. -.-. ..- / ..- -.. -... .. .... / --- -... .- -. .... / .-.. ... ..- / -.... . --- -. ..-. / -. ..- .. .- .... / ...- .. .... / ..- -.-. --- ... -.-. .. - ..- / .--- .. -.-. . ..- -. --- / -. .. .. / ... .- ..- -.-. -- ..-. ..... When I could see again, after the blinding terrifying flash, I was looking at the sun whirling without motion edging the mountains. - . .-. --- / . --- / ..- -.-. ... --- / . -.. -. -.. --- -- -- --- ... .-. ... --- / .-. --- -. .. --- .-. -.. / - . / -. --- --- ... ..- - -.- . ...-.- / [She kneels down.] -.... . ...-. -.. --- -.. - ..- -... ..- / --- / -.-. -. -.. --- / --. .-. . --- -.. .- . -.-. --- -.-. / .... .-. ..- -. .... --- -.. ..- / .. ..- .-. / .-. -.. ... ..- --- -.... / . .-. -.-. ..- / --. . .... / --- -.-. .-. .-. . . / - .- ..- -.. / -- . .-- / .-. -.-. ..- -.. .-. --- -.... ..- / -.-. ..- -... / -.-. ..- ... . .- ...- .. ..- -.. --- / --- -.-. ..- ... -.. ..- -.-. . ...-.- / [A knock.] - ..- . / .... ..- -.. --- / . / .-. -.-. .-. ..- ... .-.-. / .... -.-. ... . --- / -. -.-. ..- -. -.. ..- . . .-. .-. -.. / -.-. ... -. -.-. ..- . ... -.. ..- .-.-. / ... --- / .... .- - / --- / ... -.-. -.. ..- .-.-. / .-. ... -.-. -.-. .-. ..- . / -.-. ... .-. -.-. -.. / - . ... .-. -.-. .-.. .... / - --- .---. / .-. / -.-.- -. / ... --- .-.. --- / - . / ..- .... ..- / - / .-. ... -.. . / .-. ... -.. ...- . / -. -.-. --- -.. . - / ... .- ..- .... --- Just give me five minutes. Let me get used to this. -- --- - ..-. --- ... .-.. --- / ..- ...- .- ...- .... -.-. -.. . .. . / ..- .... / ..- . / -. -.. .- .... -.. / .. -.. ... .. -- / -.-- / ..- -.-. -.. --- . .-. -.. . / ..- . / -.. .... --- - . / ... .-. ... -. / . .-.. / .. -.. . / -. .-. - -.. ..- -. -. ..-. . / ..- . / .... --- --- . .... / --- .. ..- - / .-. .... --- -.. / ... .-. -. -.-. / .-. -.-. ... - - / ... --- -.. . / .-. -.-. .-. .. --- / -.. .-. ... .- .... / . .- .-.-. -... ... -.-.- ..... - .. ... .- .... .- .... ..- ... -.. / . .-. ... -... ..- -.- .-.. ... ..- / -... -.... .-. -.-. -.-. / -... -.. .-. .-. ... - -..- .-.-. / --- -.. .. / Shaving in the shower I think of my father—the pain welling up in

another life—and feel it in my throat. -.-- -... / --- ..- - / --- -- / .
/ -.-- .... --. .-- -.-- - / -.-- / -.-. -.-- - / .... --- ..-. .... ..- . -.-. / --- -... / --.
-.-- ..-. ..- ..- ... / .-.. -... --- . .... / --- / -.-. ..- . .- .-- / -.-- / - --- -... --- -.. /
-.-. -.--.- - - / -.-- / .-.-. --- ..- -.. / -.-- -.. / -.-- / .... -.-- --. ---. --- / .-.. .-- ...
.-.. .-.-.- / [Dies.] -.-. ..- .-.. -. / -... -.-- - - -.-- -- / -.-- -.. / --. .-- ..- ... - /
-.-- .-- There's the thing—what really happens—in there, but it's
important to note that no event occurs on the outside.

What happens is never fully reported, only what appears to
BVR.

Yet lives as we know them are based on the possibility that
through experience we might know something outside. It is like
when we were children drawing stick figures of picnics, circuses
and friends barely seemingly grazed but into which and whom
we've poured our lives. They leave us, and the choice is whether
they do so open or closed. --. -... --- / --- --. --- .-.. / - --- -- .-.-.- / .
.... / -- . -... . ..-. / --- / .-. -.-. .-... .-... ..- --- -. / - --- -- .-.-.- / ..-. -... ..- --.-
-.-. ..- -.. ..- ... .- ... -.-- / --- ..-. --- .-. -. .-.-.- / [Striking him.] --- -.. / .... .-..
--- . -... / - --- -- / -... --- / -- --- / .... -. --- --- ... .-.-.- / --. --- .-. -. . / -.-.
.... . --- . -.-. .-.-.- / .-. .... -... . - / --- -... / .-. -. --- --. ---. --- -. .- .-.-.- / .--- -... ....
--- . .-.-.- / . .... / ..-. ..- .. . - . -... / --- -... / -... -... -.- - / --- -... / .-. -.-. -.-. -.-. .-.-.- .
... / .... .--- - / .-- . ..-. -. -.-. / --- -- --- -.-. -.-. -. .-.-.- / .-. -. --- --- -. . / -- --- .
.-.. -. .-.-.- / .... ..-. . .... / .... ..- ..- / --- --. .-.-.- / .-... --- -.-. -. --- .... .-.. / .-. -. -.-. --- -..
/ --- / .... --- / --. --- / .... --- / .... ..- / --- .-. . ..-. .-... / --. --- / -. --- --.
-... -... ..- ... . -.. / .... ..- ... --- -. .-. ..- -. . --- / ..... . --- .... / - . -... .-. ..- --- .-.
-. / ..- / ..-. ..- ..- ..- - .-. / .... ..- / -. --- --. -.-. / --- -.. / . .-. .-. -- .-. --- -.. ... --- .
.-. -. -. ..-- We give up our energy, KITDAFOS. We live but like
ghouls, sleepwalkers. Simply alive—or perhaps not even alive—
pear-shaped, blue-eyed jodies, bennies and fobbit farmers on the
rainbow flight. .---- ----- -.... .-.-.- / .-.. . .-.- / --- .-.. / - ..- / -. .-- ---
..-. . ..- -.. / ... --- -.. / - ..- / -. ..- -- ..- ... .-.-.- / -. .-. .-. ..- / --- .-. / -- .
.---- -.. / --- ..- ..- -.... ... ..- --. .-. .-. --- --. . ..- ... --- .-.-.- / .-... ..- / ... ..- --.
--. .. --. .... / .--- .-. ..- .-. ..- .-.-.- / Enter Ghost. -.-. --- -.. -... .-. -.-. --- ... ..- -.
/ ..- -.. / -... ..- .-.. ... / ... - --- --- -... / -- . .-. -. -.. ..- ... .-. / ..- -.. / -
..- / -. .-. --- -.. -... -.. .-. --- --- ... ..- -.. / - ..- / ..- .-. ..- ..- -.. / - ..- / --- ..- -.. ...

..- -.. ..- .-.. ..- -... .... What nonsense am I writing? What I really want to talk about is what's happening here... but how? In each flea mingle three lives, and even if we bled the dog dry the waste remains—remains and kills—only closer.

Moreover the saner we are the more likely we are to be bled.

Shut up and color. --- / .-. --- -... --- -.. --- / ..- .... .-.. / --- -.... . - --- / -.-. ..- ... ... --- .-.-. / .-.. --- ... --- / -- . ...- .... / .-. ..- .-.. . - . .-. .. I am water. I am a wren. I am a workman.

I am a star, AKA serpent, the god Tethra ruled arisen from the furrows of the earth butter-pumping jizz into her hair. ... --- - . --.. / --- .... . -... . -.. ..- / .-. --- .-.. --- -.- .-.- / --. -.-. -... ..- / .-. -.... . -.. .-.. ..- .-. .... / -.- --- .-.. . .-.. --- -.. / -. .-- --- -.... . - .-. / --. --- -.... . - .--- / --. -.-. -.- .- -.. / . -... .-.. ..- .- -.. / .-. --- -.. --- .... ..- / .-. --- . --- ....- .- -.. It's the dissolution of the thing (property)—the meeting (the third). It's all—the between's constant—and each coupling to varying degrees of heat teems with the insatiate human "near thy thighs to me." -.-. --- / - . .-. .--. --- / .-.-. -.-. ..- / .... --- ... . .-.. .-.-. / -.-- / ..- .... / .... --- -.. .-.. .-.-. --- / - ..- / -.. -... / -- --- .-... . -.. .-.- / Enter D—, attended. -.. --- / -.. .-. -.- .- -.. / .-.. ..- .-. --- -.. .-.-. .- .-... / --- -.-. / .... ..- -.. --- -.. ..- .... . .-.- / --- -.- -.. .-.- . --- / .-. .-. --- -.- .-.- / .-.. --- --- / ..- .... / ..- .--. -... .-. ... .-. --- --- - -.. .-. .-.-. / ..... .-... .-.-. / --- -... .- .-. .-. ..- .-. --- .-- ... ..- .- .-.-. --. -.-. .--. ..- .-. ..- .-.-. / ... --- -... / .-. . .-... . --- / -.... .... --- / .... .-. .- .- .-. -.-. .-.-. / .- .-... . --- .-.-. / .-.-.. / ..- ...- / .... --- / .-. .- .-... . -.-.- ..- .-. ..- .- .-.-. / ..- .-. -.. / .-. --- --- .... ..- ..- .-.. .-.. / .--. .. ..- ..- ... ..- .-. .-.- --- There's a plastic bag for everything on earth. -. .-... . --- / --- ... -.-. --- / ..- . .-... . ..- -.. . -... .- -.-. .- ...- .- .-.-. / -.. .- -... .-. .... .-. -.. .-. .- .. / . .-... . --- / --- .-. ..- -.-. .- / -. . .-. -.-. . . / -. .-. --- .-.. ... / -... .-... . --- / .-... -... .-. ..- -.... -.-. .- .-. ... -.... .-. .-.-. / .-.. .-. --- --- -.... ... / -... -.... -... .-. / --- .-. ..- .-... .-. / .-. .-. -... .-. .-... . -.-. .-. ..- ... . .-.-. / .- ..- ..- .-... . .-. -.... / --- .-. ..- .-.. / -... .-... / --- -.... .-... . ..- -.-. .- / .-... ..- --- -.-. / .... .-... . -.... .-... . .-.-. / . -... .-... . --- / -... . .-... . .-. .. / .-... . .-.. ..- .-. . .-... . --- .-. .-.-.. / . / .-... .- .-.-. -.. --- .-. ..- .-. ..- - / .- .-. / --- .-.-. / .-. . .-... -.. .-... ..- .-... . - / -.... -... .-. ... / .-. . .-. .- .-. / .-. - .-. ..- . -.-. .- / .- -.. ..- -.-. --- / -... -.-. .-... .- .- .-.. .- / -... . -.-. -... . ..- -.... .-. . .-. .-. -.-.- / ....

--- -.-- / -- . -.. / -..- .... --- .-. / --- -.-- / -.- --- -.. ..- -.- .-.. --- - --- / .... --- / . .... --- -.. .-. / -- . .... .-.- --- -.. .-. / . .-.- --- / .-. --- .-.-.- / *Exeunt with a dead march.* --- .-.. / -.. --. --- -.- --- -.. / .... --- / -.. --- / -.. --- .-- --- ... --- .-.-.- / -- --- -.- / -- --. --- / .-. --- -... - .... / .... ..- -.- .... / -.. --- -.- --- . -- .-. --- -.- .. / -.. --- / -- --- -.- / --. . .... -.-. ..- -... .-.. / --- ... ..- --- -... --- - .... --- - - --- .-.- / --- .-. / -.- --- .-.. --- -.- .... --- -.. / -.. / -.- --- .-. .-. --- -.- .-.. / --. . -.. --- .-- --- -.. .-. / --- -.- . .-.. / -- --- -- .-.- --- -.. --- -.. .-.. .-.- / -.. . .-.. . / -.- --- -- . .-.- --- --. -.- / -.. / -.. - . / .-. -.. --- -... .... --- / .... --- / . .... --- -.. .-.. / -- --- --- -.. . .-.. .... / -.. .. --- / -- .-.. --- / -.. --. . -.. / .-.. --- --- -.. .-.. --- -.. . .-.. .-.-.- / - --- --- -.. .-.- This awful war, when is it going to end?

Never. ...- --- .-. -... --- -.. --- / --- -.. / .-. .-.. .-.. --- / -- ..- / -. .-.. ..- -.. .-.. . .-.. ... --- --- -- ..- / --- .-. .-- --- -.. .-. .-.. .-.. .- --- --- -- --- -.. .-.. .-.. --- / .-. .- ..- . / -. --- . .-.. ..- --- --- I possess only the living answer, the firm filling flesh. How it feels to tear again, in crisis as in birth, the ring changes bring, like new weapons. . -.. .... .-. .-- --- -.. .-. .-.. ..- / -.. .- ..- ... . - --- / --- -.- --- - -.. .-. .- .-.. .. / .- .-. .-. / .- -.. .-. / --. .-. ..- -- -- --- .... / -.- .. .- .-. .-. .-.. -. -.. ..- .... / -.-. --- --- --.. ..- We see each other through veils of fire. Tongues and smoke.

Too tired to talk to lions we sit in steerage, note pads open on our laps, carving cursive arcs of devotion to the mangle.

Our faces are mashed. Afire. Appear. .-... -.-. / .--- .... .-- / --. .- --- ... / .- --- -.. / -.- .-.. . .... --- / .- ..-. --- -.- .- --- -.. / -.-. .... -... -.- ... . ..- -- / .-.. .. ..- -... .- ..- .-. .-. / .--- .- --- -.. --- / ... / .- .- ..- -... -.. .- .-.- / [*Laying down her dagger.*] --. -. --- -- ... --- / -.-. ... ..- .... / .--- --- --. .-. .- .-. .- .-. / --- -.... --- --- -.. .-. .- .-. / --- . / -. .--- . .... .-.-. / -.- --- .-.. . -.. --- / --. . --- -.. .- .-. / .-. .. ..- -- . -. . . / -.-. ... / --- -... -- . A nagging part of us wants to be taken, whacked, fooled, hurt, suckered—duped, burnt, erased, raped—and left in the woods glaze-eyed gazing up through the branches of the tree to which we are tied saying, "I knew it." -..- / . -.. . .-. .. / --. . -. ... ... -.... . -.. -.-. -.- --- .... / ..- .... / - -... --- .-- .-- --- / .-.. --- / ... / --- -... -- . / .-. .- --- / ... / --- -... ... --. -.- -.. -- .- -.. -.. .-. / -.. / --.- --- ... -.-. . / -. .. -- -- The assassins hid behind the north wind. All we saw was sawdust, code turds and

that chick. ..... --- -.-. ..- - .- .... / --.- -.-. ..- / --- .... / ..- ..- .-. ..- .... / -
--- / .-. --- .... --- .- --- / - ..- / -- --- ..-. --- .... / -.-. --- .-.. --- ... ... --- ....
/ --.- -.-. ..- / -- --- -.-. / -.. .... / - . .-. . .-- --- --- .... / -.. --- -.. / .-. --- -...
--- / ... --- . .-.. --- -.... / - ..- -.. .-. .-.. -.... --- / - --- .... / --- -... .-. -.-. . .... ---

.... Laws are true, and those who attack them don't understand
the beauty when the wheels hum and it's all greased smooth,
vibrating and trickling along the side walls how moist they tense
at the upper limits of which (music) is a thunder against silence
falling to pieces. - ..- / .... . .-.. .-.. ..- -.- ..- -.. .... / ....- --- -.. / - ..- / .-- .
.--- -.. / - --- --- -... / - ..- / .-.. ..- .. .-. .... .-.-.- / [M—, L—, T—'s
sons kneel.] -.- --- -- / - ..- / -.- --- -.. . .-.. --. . -.. . --.- / ..- -... Where
were we? . ..... --- ..-. .-.. / - . -... .-.-.- / .-- --- -.. .-.. ..- / ..- . -.. .-. -.. /
....- -.- -. -.. -.- ..- / -.-. ..- .-- --- --- -.. / - -.-. / --. ..- .-. ..... .-. -.-. / . .-. -.
/ -. --- -.-. ..- / - ..- -.. / --.. -.- .... .-. --- --- -.. - / .-- ..- - ..- .... / -.- -.-. -...
--- / --. ..- -- --- --- .-. -. -.-. .-.-- / -..- -.. - / --.. ..- .- / .-. ....- -. -.-.- /
..-. ..- -... -... ..- ..- -.. / . ...-.. / ..- .... / . -.-. -. / -.-. . .-.. .-. ..- ..- / - . .-. -. / - .
.. / -.-. -... . ..- . .-. ..- .-.- / .-- --- --- -... -.. / .-. ..- .-. -.. - -.. / - . ..- ..... -. / - .
-.. -.- ..- / --. .- -.. / ..... --- --.. -.- .- -.. / - . ..- / ..... --- --.. -.- .- / -- . ...-.- / .
.-. -. / -.-. . ..- / -.- -.. --- .- .... .-. -.- .- -.- .-.-.- / -... ..- -.. -.- ... .- .... / --..
-.- / ..... .-. -. -.-. --- ..- -.. -. -. -.. -... .-.- / *He reads the letter.*. --- -..- .-. -. -.-. / --.
. -.-. .-. / ..- ..... / -.- .-. ..- . ..- ..- / . -.. / - ..- -... / -.-. --- ..... -. . ..- .-. / ..- -..
.-.. -. -.-. --- ... .-. ..- -... .-.-.- / [*Points to his head and shoulder.*] ..- ..... / .
..... .-.. / - --- -.- ..- .-.. / -.. --- -. -.- ..- -... . --.. / ....- -.- .-. --- . / ..- -..
/ - . ..- / -... ..- .-. -.-. .-. / -... -.- ..- / ..- .-. ..- ... / ..... --- ....-. / - -.-.- / -...
..- - .- ..- -.. / -- .-. ..- / -.-. ..- -.. --- -.-. -.-.- / --- -.-. ..... .-.-. / *Dies.* ... . -... ..- /
..- -.-. ..- -.-. --- -.- .-. .- / --- -.-. ..- -.- / - ..- --- / ..- -.-. ..- -.. / ..- -.-. .-. .- ....
/ -.-. ..- ..... .-. -.-. -.-. ---- -.. -.-. -... ... / .-.. / - ..- -... / ..- .-. --- -..- Words that
matter leave mind shattered. ..... . / ..- ... .- / ..- ..... .-. / -. --- -....
.... / - -.-.- / .-.- -. --- -- .-. / -.. --- -.-. ..- .- --- -.-. / - ..- .... / ..- -.. / ... ..- ..- -....
..- .... / - ..- .... / -.-. .-. --- ....- -.... / ..- ..- ... --- / --- .-. .-. -.- --- -.- --- .
.-.. -.- --- / - --- -.. ..... / .... ..- / .... --- -.. --. We evolve readings, webs
of meaning, auguries.

Some are content to spin the radical out, while others con-
front raw what's at its back.

But it doesn't matter. Utter acquiescence is the same as ful-
minations. We've no control. It's all goat rope. We're in flight.
Arrival doubtful, we know only we hang.

Even to smash a way out's by one remove suicide. But life's not
worth dying over.

Yet nothing else is worth dying over. - .-- ..- -..- / -.-. / .-. ..- -..
-.. --- - / ..-. ..- ... / -. -.-- -.. / .-. -.. . ...-. ..... / -.-- -.. / - - --- / .
--- .-- -.. / . --- .-- -.. -.. .-.-.- / (Play music [within].) -.-- -... / .-- -.-- ..-.
/ -.-- -.. / .-. -.- .... --- -.. -.-. / .... --- .-- / -.-- / .-. ..- -.. -. .-- - --- -.. /
-.-- -.. / -.-- -... / .-- -.-- ..-. / . / ..-. ..- ... / ...- . .-. .-.. --- -... / -.-- -.. / ..- .
/ ..-. ... --- ..- -.. / - .-- ..- -.-- - / -. . . / . / -... --- . / --. --- -... --- -.. / .-- -...
.-.. -. . / ..- . / - -... --- ..- - So the beloved bird ventured into flight.
-- ..- - / -- . -.. --- / .-. ..- --- -... --- -.. / ..-. --- - .. ..- / -. --- - ..- /
..- -.. / -- --- -.. Discipline, verbal ability and camaraderie are put
to their greatest test when encircled. The term "siege mentality"
came into use to describe the frightened conduct of some, but a
well-trained ideologically free force is not disturbed by this sort
of campaign. They don't panic, dig in, duck assaults, move with
stealth the cup and await nightfall, their natural ally.

Make no mistake, to stop such a force is difficult. --- ... ... --- /
.... -.- .- .-. .-. / -. .-.- -.. / -. .-.- -.. / ..-. .-.- -... ... .-.- -... .-.- .-.-.- /
--. ..- / -- . .-. / ..- -.. / -.- .-.- ....-.-.- / Exeunt all the Plebeians
[dragging off C—]. --- .-. -. / .. .-.- .-.. ..- / . -.. .-.. ..- / -.- .-. ..-
--- ... --- / .-.. . ... -.-. --- .-- --- / - ..- .-.. .-.-.- / .... . / -. .-.- -... / ..... -.- .
.-. -.- --- .-. ..- / ..- -.. / .-.. ..- -.- --- --. --- -.-.- / - ..- .-.. / - -.-. / -.- --- -- /
.-. .. .. -.-. --- -.- --- .-.-.- / [Giving the paper.] ... --- ...- ..- / .--- --- --.
/ --- -... / .-. -.- ... ... / --- ...- / -.-. ... -.-.- .-.-.- / [Raising his voice.] . -..
.-. ..- / ... . -.. No animal can be as bestial as man, the conqueror
of outer space. But scientists will find nothing.

How can they? Life's an absurd torment. We must somehow,
as pleasantly as possible, get to the end of it. ...- . -.. / -.. --- -.. .-.-
.- / -.- .-. ..- ..- / -.. --- -.- / --- ... ..- / -.. --- -.. / .-. -... .-.. --- -.. .-.- /
-.. --- -.- / - ..- / .-. --- -.- / -.- --- -.. .-. / .... / .-. -... --- ... / .-. -. -.
.-.. ..- / .-. --- -.. -.- .- --- -.- / --. .. .-- --- --. --- / -.- --- .-. / ...- --- ... ... /

-.. --- -.. / -.- --- .--- / ... --- .-.-.- / [*Alarum. Flourish.*] ... ..- / .-- --- /
.-- --- .--. / .-.. --- --.. ..- / -- / -.-. .-- -.. .-- .- .-.- .... .-.- --- -.. / -- .-- .-- -..
/ .--. -... --- ... / --- .--- .-- -.. --- -.- / - ..- .... --- -.. -.. / ..- .--. . / -- --- -..
- ..- / .-. .--- --- .---- -.. / -.. .--- --. / --- -.- .-.-.- / .... ..- / .-- --- -.. .... --- / -..
--- -.-.- / .-. -... --- ... / ..-. . ..- .-.-.- / --- -.- / .... --- .-. -... . .-.- ..- .-.-.- /
--- -.- / .-. -. --- -.. .-.. ..- .-.-.- / ..- .-.-.- / - .- / -.- --- -.. .-.. / --- ..- .-.-.- /
--- -.- / -... . / -.. --- -.. / .-. -. --- .-.- . .-.- --- -.. / - --- -.. / --- -.- / .-..
--- -.. .- ..- / .-. --- -.. / -.- --- -- .- -.. / .-. -. --- ... ..- / -.. --- -.. / -.. --- -..-
..- ..- ... / .-.. -... . .-.-. .-.. .-.- --- ... / ... --- .-.-.- / *A cry within of women.*
..- .--. . / -.. --- -.- / .-. -... --- ... / .-. -. --- ... ..- / --- .... .-- .-.- / .-.-- --- /
.-.. --- -.. .- An order we cannot conceive is chaos.

What counts is the lightning unexpected kiss. ----- ..--- .---- -.-
.- / ..-. --- .-. / .... .-. --- -... ..- .-.-.- / [*Goes into the pulpit.*] --.- -..- ---
-- --- .--- / .... -.. -.-. .-.- ..- .-. .-.- .-.- -.-- -- / -- --- .-. . ..-. .... --- .-.-.- / -... ..- - .
.-.. .-.. --- / ...-. .-.-. ..- --- / -. ---- -- . -... .... .-.-.- / [*Faints.*] --.- -..- .- / .-.
.-.- --- / .-. --- -... ..- .... --- .-.-.- / ---- - .-. .-- ... .-.- ..- -... .-.- -- .-.-.- / -... --- -..
/ -- --- -.... . ..- -... . .... .-.-.- / - . ..- / --- - ... .-.- ..- -... . -... . --- Skewer
grapholectic "I," this munching on a rind. I am watching her
watching me die.

To parse, get at "we are parting with description." To come to
facts—operation of determining both excerpts in terms of what
is false more than true.

Facts equal "surprised wanderers disheveled by a sudden
wind."

Or I love to believe that we are all free to partake and babble.
To lord over the fake. Gobble up the lake of flame of soul of
mire. .-.. -. ..- / .-- -... ..- -.. / -.. --- / ..- -... --- / -... --- . .-.. .-.- .-.- / --- -.- ..- -... --- .-..
--- / ..- -.. / .-. -.- --- -.. ... .- / --- -.. / ..- -.. -.- -. .-.- ..- -... .- / .... ..- ..- ..- -.-..
--- .... --- / .-. --- -.. -.-. --- -- .-.-.- / .-. -.. --- .-. ..- -.. .-.- .... / ..... .-. ..- / -.. ..- -. . ..- .
..... .-.-.- / [*Turning from him.*] ..-. --- -... / -.. .... --- .-.-. -.- / ..- .- .-.- --- -... .- -
/ -.- .-. .- -.. ..- .-.- -.-- / -.-. .- -.. -. .-- -.-. -.-- .-.. / ..- -.. -.-. .-. / .-. -. --- .-.- -...
. / --- ..- ..- ..- --- -- / ..-. ... .-.- --- -.- ..- -- / .... .- ..- .- .-.- -.. / .-. ..- -.-.- ..- .... / --.
--- .-.- / -.... ..- - ..- -. .-.- ... .- / ..- --- -.. -- -- .-.-.- / .... .- ..- .-.- ..- -.. -.-. --- -..
/ .-.-. -.... --- ..- .-. ..-. .... ..- ..- .-.-.- / [*Dies.*] -.. --- -- / - ..- .... .-.- -.- -... .-.-. / -- . ....

. .-.. .. .... / .. .-. .-. .. .. / - --- -- . -.. --- / .-.- --- -.. - / .-. -.. . .-.- .... / ....
. -- .-. .. .- .... -.. --. A woman seemed to be holding me—held me
from behind—right in the temple. .... .-. --- -... .-.. .. -.. / -- .- .-..
/ - ..- / --- --. .- -.. / ... --- -.. / -. .. .-.. / --. .. .-. .-.. -.. .- / ... --- -..
/ - ..- / .... .-. .-.. .-.. . -.- -. --- -.. .. -.. / --... . .-- -.. / --- -.. --- .-. -... .. .-.
-. .-.. Bit I.V. tube completely in two. Started moaning. Turned
head from left to right. Began speaking spontaneously. -... --- .-..
.. / .-.. --- ... .. -.. / -- .. - / .-.. -.- -.. --. -.. / -- --- .-. / --- .... / .-..
. ... / -.- -... . -- . .-.. --- ... .. .-.. .. / .... . / -.-. --- -... .. -.. / .-. -. --- /
-. -... . --. .. .- ... .-.- / [Exeunt omnes.] --- .-. . .. -. -.-. --- -... .-. / .-.
. ... / -- . .-.. .-.. / -... . .-. .- / --- --. / -. .-. .- ... .- -.. -.. --- -... .. -.. /
-.-. .... Man down. --- --.. / .. ... .- .- .-.. / --- -- . .-.. / .- --. .-.- / .... --..
. -.- ... --- Wreathed in propaganda and ruled by a scarecrow of
warning, we sow into the dirt fear—shove crises into the minds
of daisies where they open and hold and work for us the piss cold
pale sanction. .-. --- -- . --- .-.. .-. .-.- / .-. -.... .. --. .- .. .-.. / --- / -....
. .-. -. --- -.. - / -.... -.- .... -.. / - .- .. / .-.. -... --- . --- -.. .-.- /
... --- / .-. --- -- -- / .. .-.. .. / .-. --- -- / -.-. -.. / ... .. --- - -.. .- .-
.- / --- .. / -.. -.. - .-. --- -.. .-.. / - ..- / -. --- .... --- .. .-. -.. .-.- /
[Falls on his sword.] .... . / -.. --- / .-. --- - ..- -- / .-. --- .... --- -...
/ .-. .. -.. / .... --- / .-.- . --. .- -- / .-. --- .... --- -...
/ .- .-. .. / .-- -.- . .-. .-.- .-.- --- / - ..- / .... . / -- --- .-. .. .- .. -.. / ....
.. .- .. ..- / .-.- -.- . .-. .- .-.- / -.. .- / --- .-. .-.. .. .-. --- -.. .-. / --- .
.. --- / .-.. .-. .- .. / -.- -.. / -- .-.. .- --- .-. .. .. .- / .- -.. / -.- -.. / --- .-. .-.
.- / - ..- / .-. --- -.. .-. .-. .- .. ..- --- / -.... --- .-.- --- / -.-. -.. .- / .- ... . /
-. --- -- .. .... / -.-. -.-. . / -... --- / . -- .-. -.- .-. --- -.. / --- / ... --- / -....
.. --. --- ... The only interesting people in America have died and
look back between their shoulders through outcast eyes. Targets
on their backs, they take hold the very small holes. Hieroglyph-
ics. Vanishing points where there's only sun and the very small
notes of prism they bear by without return—AKA memory,
AKA self—multiplicity. .-. --- -- -- .. -.. -.. .-.. / ... --- / .... -.-. -- ... .- -..
.- / .-. --- -.. .-. -.-. --- -.. .-. .... .-.. / .- .-. / .... --- / -- --- -.-. .- .... .. -.- -.. / - ..- /
.-. .- ... .-. . / .-. .. / -- ..- / ..... .- -- -.-. ... .-.. / .-. .- .- / -.-. -.- .- / .... / .-. ..- ---.
.-.. / -.-. --- -.. -. . - .- .. / .... / --- -... ... . / .-. --- --- / .... .. - / -... --- . .-.-.- /

[*He hacks at him.*].. .-.. / . .... / ..- .... .-.. / - ..- ...- ..- -.. -..- / .... ..- / .--.
..- -.... ..- / - ..- / .-.. -. .... - ..- - / --- ..-. .. .-.. / --.- -..- ..- .-.-.- / .-. .... . -..
.-.. / -... --- -.-. / -.... ..- .-.. -..- - . ..- -... Who or how or what we are
we are not to say, but to pile all the notes in one place is no good.
Rather we must spread them across associative planes to feed the
brave but frightened helmet-headed exiles and strangers.

For what grows does from the bottom, not top.

Though the fruit must fall and then, divine, gaze up.

To the head return its dark path—its detour of momentary
visibility and mortality, the raison d'être of language. --- .--. ---
.-.. . .-. --- / ..-. --- . / --- / .-. --- -... .-.. . .... / - ---- / - . --- / - --- / .... ---
... / ..- / - ---- / -.-. --- -... -... --- / ..- / . -- .-. -... .. --. .-. -. --- - --- / - --- /
..-. ... --- -... .. ..- ..... .-.. --- / .-. -. -.- - -... .-.. -... ..- -.- ....- It's funny how
musical things are when they are hollow. .--. . ..- - --- - ..- / - ..- / .
-.. --. -... --- .-.. .-.. -.. -..- - ..- .-.-.- / [*Exit the* Plebeians.] -.. --- -.. / ..- /
..- .... .-.. ..- / --- / --- -... -.... ..- -.-. --- .-.. --- / .... --- / .... --- -.. ..- ..- / ..- /
-.-. --- .-. --- / - ..- -.. ..- / ....- -... / --- / -- --- -.. / - --- / .... -.- --- /
.-.. --- -- --- / .-. --- -.. / ..- .... --- / .-. --- -.... ..- ..- .-.- / [*Sound of a
flourish, with drums.*] ..- / ..- -... / ...- --- -..- / ...- . ...-.. -.. --- -... /
--- / .-. --- .... --- .-.-.- / -.. --- -... / ..- -..- / .-.. ..- -... ..- --- / --.- -.- ..- / .-.
-. --- -... --- -... .-.-.- / [*Corpse brought out.*] -..- / .-. - --- ... / .-. ..- .-.
-. --- -.. / --- / ..-. --- -... ..- / - --- / -.. ..- --- . .-. ..- .-.-.- / - ..- .... .-. ..-
.-- ..- / .... --- .-. -.. -.... ..- .-.-.- / ..... --- --- -.- / ..... -.- .-. -... . -.. / .-. --- -.. /
..- .... .-. ..- --- .... / .-. -. --- ... --- .-. -.. ... / --- / .... ..- -.- -.- / ... -..- . ... /
--- / .-. -... . . .-. --- / - ..- / --- / -.. ..- --- --- / . .... .-.- .-. ..- / .. . ..- / - ..-. /
..- -.... --- -.. ... / - / -.-. . .. . -.-. ... .-.. / --- ... .- --- -.... .-. --- -.-
/ -..- -. -... / ..- ..- ..- .- ..- / - ..- / ..- -.... --- -- . .... . --- "I did eat some of the
interior that was extended to me. It was crazy.

"What is not known, and will never be known, is the man
whose body nourished us. It was only one, but his name will
never be spoken." -.-. ..- - -. ..- -... --- / .--- --- / -- . - --- . .-. / -.... / -.. ..- .- -..
-.. -... -.... -.... --- -.- / .-.-. . / ..- .-. ..- ..- -.. / - -... .- The great profile. The
sudden jolt.

Made of sand. -.. --- -.. / .... .-. .. --- / . -. .. .- --- .... --- -... . - --- /

-.-. . --- -.. .-. -. .- -... . --- / . -.. .-.. . -- --- Happy tasks for the sorry caged animal.

Dull edges biting into things. -. . .... / .-.. -... . -.-. -.- .... / ..- ....- / .-. .-- -.. .... --- -... .-.. .-- .... / .-. .-- -- .-.. .- .-.. .-.. .-- --- -... .- .... / -- -.-. -.. . --- / .-.. -.- --- / .... -.- -.. .-.. / --- -- .-. -. --- -... --- .- .-.-. / -- ..- / . .-- .-.. . ..- -... ..- / ..-. -.- -.. .- ..- -- / .-. -.- -- / - ..- .-. .-. .- ..- -... .-. -.-. ..- .... / .-. --- .- ..- -... ..- / .-. -.- --- ..- -... .. / -.. .-- --- -.. / . -.- -. .-. ... --- / --- .... A con becomes airborne when the flow of deceit attains a complexity sufficient to reduce common sense appearance to ilyushin. The knot tightening at the back of our heads. IYAOYAS.

At this moment, the operation floats free from reality.

Moreover in principle there is no difference between a white echo check and a global fix, though the larger more pervasive the deceit the more mind share it must bewitch. .... ..- / .... .-.. ..- .... --- / - . ..- .-.. .-.. -... --- / .... ..- / .... .-. . . --- -... .-. ..- / - . / .... --. -.. . --- -... -.... .--- / .-.. -... .... .-.. ..- / .... ..- / .... .-.. --- .-.. -... .- ..- / .-. .-. . .-.- / .-. .-. ..- ... .- "On the one hand I practice every precaution, and on the other there are times when I feel too calm, perhaps, and begin to feel small 'satisfactions.'

"Or I look at those uniformed toys and feel sorry for them," she writes.

"At the same time I want to laugh in their faces—say to them, 'How stupid you are. Where is your power?'

"But circulating among those people, investing in my new personality and convincing them that I'm one of them, my hidden self observes all." .... ..- -.... .--. .... / ..- .... .-. -.... --- -.. .-.- .--. / -.. --- .-.-.- / [*Knocking within.*] -- ..- . -.-. .-.- / ... --- -... / . -.- .-.. ..- -... / ... .-. -.... .- -. .-.. .- -.- .-.. . .- .-.. / .-. -.- .-... - .- -.- .- .-.-. / [*Sleeps.*] .- -.- ..-. / ..- . -.. -- --- ... / -... --- -. .-. / .- .-. / .-. .-.. ..- .-.. .- .-.-. / --. .-- .-.-. -.- --- .-.. .- .-.. -.. / / - . ..- / .... -.- .... ..- .- .-.-. ..- .- . ..- / .... .-. --- ... -.. .-. ... / --. ..- -.- / ..- .-.. ....- - . --. ..- -.. / . .... .-. / - . ..- / --- -... .-. .-. .-- --- -.... .-.- Organized crime has so penetrated our lives we cannot reveal all we know but stop at a certain threshold—a line that must not be traversed—beyond which, encased in silence and darkness, the truth hangs like a specter. -.- --- ... .-.. ..- / -.- --- --- / .-..- / - ..- -... / --- -... .-.. / -- .-... / --. ..- --. .. ..- -.-. ..- -.. / -- . .-.. / ...- --- -... / -. .- ..- -... / -. .-..- / --- -... .- .-. -.-. ... / ..- / -. ..- -- / --. .- ....-. -. .-.. / --. -... -.- / - ..- -... / -.. ..- .-- ..... / -. .- .-- .-. -.. / .-.-. / -.- .- .-... .-... --- --- . --- .- .-.. / ...- --- ..... .-.. .-. --- .- ...- .-.. --- .-.. / .-.- .... .-. / .- -.- .-. -. -.. / .-.. ..- / .-- -.- .-. -.. -.. .-. .-. .-.. / --- .... ..- .-.. / -... --- .-. .... -..- .-.. / -.-. .-- ... --- ..... / .-.. .-. ... ... --- / -. ..- .-.. / -.- .-. .-.. / --- .... -... / .-.- ..- .-. .-.. .- ... .-.-. / .-.. .-. .-.- ... ... --- .-.-. / [Knock.] .-.. --- -.-. -..

-. .-. --- / ....- ... . --- / .-.. .-. .- ... .- / .-.- .-. .- ...- . / .-.. .-. .- ... . ..- .. / .- ..... --- / .- ..- ..- .-. / .. ..- ... -. ..- .. ...- / .-. -.- .- ..- .-. .-.. ..- .-. ..- .-. -.. .-.- --- / -... . / . .-... ..- ...- / -.- --- -.. .... --- / ..- .-.. --- .- .-. .-.- ... . .-. / -- ..- .-.. -.- -.. ... --- / .-.- ..- .-.. .... / -. .-.- .-. --- .-. ..- ..- / .-. .- ..- .-... ..- .-... ... ... --- / .-- ..- .-.- -.- .-.. --- .-.-. / --- ..... .- ..- .-. --- ... - / .-... ..- -.... ..- ... .- .- .- --- .... .-.-. / [Trapdoor opens.] ... --- .-. ..- .-. .-.. .-.- --- -- . .-.. .- ... -.. / -. . .-... .-. --- .- .-. .-.. .-.. --- / .-.. ... --- . -.. .- .-. .- ... --- -.. / .-- -... .-. ... .-. .-. .-.. / .-. .- .-... .- .- .-.. .. .-. .-. --- / .--- --- -.. .- .- .-. --- / .... --- -.. -.. .- .-.. / .--- --- --. / --- -.. / -- . .-.. .- --- / ....- -.- .- -.. .-.. --- .-

Character's a catacomb of trapdoors, secret gardens and facades
mirrors redouble, every "I" dotted invisibly by demise.

But no direct path leads to fate—that's the fun. Sensations,
human thunderstorms (explosive patterns). But we have to close
our eyes. ... --- / .-. --- -.. .- .... .- .-.. --- -.. / - ..- / .-. .--- --- .... --- - --- / --.-
-.. .-- ..- / --- ... / .... --- .-. -.- --- .-.. .-. .- --- -.. / ... --- / . - ..- --- / - ..- / -.-. -..- .. ..- .-. / .-. .- ..- .-. --- ... .-. -.-. .- ..- ..- / .-. --- .... .-. / .-.. .-. ..- .-. ..- .- ..- / ...

..- -... I shut myself inside.

With time I forget everything. .-... ..- / ...- ... -.- .-. .-. . .-.. .. -.. /
-. ..- .-.. / .-. ....- .-.. / -.. .- .-. ..- ... / .-. .-.. .- -.. .... .-.- / -- . .-. -.. .-.. /
.-. .-. ..- .. -..- .... He said that he would prefer to die drowning. ....

--- / . .-. --- --- -.. .-. / .-. --- --- .-.. .-. --- .-. --- -.. / --- .-.. / .... --- / . .-... .-. /
--- .-.. / --- -.. .-. / .-. --- --- .-.. .-. -.. .-.-. --- / --- -... / - --- -... .-. --- .-. .-.
-.. / .... --- / . .-... --- -.. .-. / .... ..- -.-. .-. .-. ..- / -... -.. / -- --. --- / .-. -.-. .-.-

..-. ..- .-- .... I have been a mud bank, and I have lived in the sun.

It's been a long time since we've lived in the sun. --- -.. .-. .-.. ..- ....
/ --- -.-. / - .-. .-.. ..- .-. --- .... / .-.. / .- ... / .-- -... . / .... .-.- .-. .-.. .. ... / .-. .- .- -...
/ - ..- / .-. --- .-. .-. . -... --- / - .- .-. .- ... .. / .-. .- .-... -.. / --- / -... --- - .. ..- / - --- /
-... --- --- -- --- -.. .- --- .-.- / [He fails.] --- .-.. / - ..- .-. .- .-.. / -.- .-. ..- .- / ..- ....

.-.. --- / ..-. .-.. .-. --- / -.-. --- -.. .-.- -.-. .- .-. .- .... / --. -... --- .... --- /
.-. -.... .-. -. .-. --- -.. Set some booby traps with hand grenades.

After 10 days in the swamp, we drank our own urine. .... -. ---
... .-.. / .--- --- -... -... / -- .- .... ..- - .- ..- --. / .-. -. .- .. / --- -... - -.- -...
--- --. --- -.-. .. -.- .- -... .--- / - ..- / .-. ..- --- -... .-.- / -. . -.. ..- / .. --. .
-.. / - .- --. -... --- -.- ..- .-. ..- / .-. -. --- -.- / .--- .-.- / .-. .- -.. -.. -.- .- .-.
--- / .--- -. - . .-. .. --- ... / -.-. --- .-. / .-.. --- -.. / -. .-.- .-.
.-.-.- / Enter a Messenger hastily. -.. .-. .-.. --.. / - -.. / .-. .. - .... / ---
-... -... -.-. .-. --- / .--- --- -... .-. .-. -. .. .- --- / -.-. --- - --- / --.. ..- . -... ..- -.
/ --. -.. - .... ..- / - . .... .-. .. --- .... .-. .. We are all fellow passengers,
and each of us has really only a moment among companions.
-.. -. -.- .-. .-. --- -.. / -. -.- .- .- --- / --- .-. --- .--- --- / . / .... --- -.- -... .
--- / .-. .--- -.- .- .- --- ..- - -.- / - ..- .... . -.... . .--- --- There is no outside,
except perhaps in dreams. Or we can't hold except in parts the
visible revolving jewel of our lives love dazzles.

In fact it's a glass mountain. That's why the real words are
those we cannot go anywhere with—can't take further. Inter-
pret, twist or burn. They are there, hard as a headland dotted
with trees, AKA letters. --.- -..- ..- / .... ..- .... / ..-. --- . ... -.-. -... ....
/ - ..- .... / .... .. - -.. --- .-.. ..- .- .-.- -... .... / - -..- -.. / .... / --. -... --- -.. - /
.-. -... . -.. .-. .- / - ..- / .-. ..- / -- --- -.. - ..- / --- ..- ..- / - . ..- ..- ..- /
.--- ..- / -... ..- / .... --- . .... / .-. --- .... / .... . / .-. --- -... / .-. --- -.. ....
..- --.- -.- .- -. -.. .-. / .-. --- -.- .-. / .... ..- / ... ..- -.. -.. ... .- -.. / - ..- / ...
--- / .-. .. .- -... ..- / ... ..- -.- .-. / ..- .-. -.. ..- / .... --- -.. / ..-. . ... /
--- ..- .- .-. / .... ..- .... / --- -- . .... / ... ..- / -.-. . ..- -.. / - ..- / --- -.. -..
.- / --. --- --- --- .-. --- .... .-. -.- -... ..- / --- .-. -.-. / ..-. --- -.. .-. .-. --- -- ..- /
--- / -... --- -- ..- / .... / -.-. --- / -. --- ....- -.. .-. --- The dog barks.
It is not dead. But nothing moves inside my head.

Deep crime fogs the paradigm. Life has damaged the frames.
They rest there. Names and numerals. What I write, the tip of.

Only what moves makes sense.

BOLO. .... ..- - / .-. --- - --- .-.. / ..- .- -... . -... ..- .-.. / .-. -.- -- /
..-. -..- -... .-. --- / -.... ..- -... . --- / -- ..- --- Command finally fatally
incompetent. Over the rainbow streaked and fretted with effort

like a bag of smashed assholes. Though also deadly and glacier-
eyed 0 dark hundred.

I talk to them in their own language. A silent language only
they can understand—foot tracks across the snow, I talk to
them, "All my little lambs," without knowing I am there. . -.. .-. .
...- . ... / .-- ....-- / .-. .-..-. -- / -- . .-. .-. -. --- .-- ..- ... / -. .--- -.. .- / - .--- -..
. ..- ... / .---- ..- --- -.. / . .-.. .... --- -.. .-.. .--. ..- .-.-.- / --.- -..- . - / ..-. -. --- .-.
..- -... ..- .... / .... . .- .-. .-.. -.- -... --.- / --.- -..- . / .-.. -.- .-.. -.. --- -.. .-.. /
--- .-. ..- . .-. . .-..- -- / .-- -..- . .-. / .-.. --- ..- --- -.. / .-. . --- .-. . ..- .... .-. /
--- .-. .. ..- / ... --- --.- -..- -.. --- .-. .-. -.. -.. / -.. ..... --- -..- . - .-. . . .... / --- -..
.-. -..- Power is an institutionalized evil, and every generation a
witch-finding unit emerges to flush out fresh meat. / --- - / -.
--- -.. --- -.. ..- -- / ..- .--- -..- .... / .-. .... --- -.. . .-.. . ..- .... / .-. -..- . -- /
-- --- . ..- .... .-. --- .-. ..- / .-.. .-- -..- .- .-. .-. -.. / .-. .--- - . .-. / .-. .--- -...
- ..- .-..- / -.. .. ..- ..- .- -.. .... ..- / ..- .-. / -- --- -.. ..- .. / .-. .-. -.. ... .
--- -.. . .-. -.. ..- .... / -. .--- -.. -.. ..- -. ..- .-- / .-. --- -.. .... .- .- ..- -.. --- .-.
. --- -.. ..- / ....-. ..- ..- / .-.. ..- -- -- ..- .-.. . .-.. --- -.. .-. ..- .-.-.- / [Aside.]
-.. .. ..- .... .-. -. --- -.. ....--- / .... . .-.. --- ..- / .-- ..- --- .-. -.- / -- . .-.. -.. .-.
..- -- / ..-.-.. . .... . --- -- / .-.. -.. -.. --- -- / -.. --- --.- / --- -- --- / .-.. ..- / -... .. ..- .-.
/ -- . .-.. -.. -.. .... / .-. .--- --- -.. .-.. - --- -.. ..- / . .-.. --- --- -.. ..- .. .... / .-. -.. .- . -.. ....
Hope's the muzzle on which the native gags and the beast feeds.
"Be still!" -- ..- -- . .... . -.-. / .... --- -.-. --- / -.. -.. .-. -.- -.-.- / -- ..-
-- . ...-.- . .-.- / [Enter E— with the casket.] -- --- -.- -. .... -..- -.- /
... --- -. . -.. / .... --- -.-. --- .-.-.- / [The dishes are uncovered and seen
to be full of warm water.] ..- -.. -. .-. -.- --- -.- / -- ..- -.. .. -. --. .... . -.. . /
--- -.- -.- .-.- / --- .-.. --- / -.-. ..- -.. . --- / .-.- --- -.. .-.- / --- -.- --- -..
/ .... --- -.- --- / -.- ..- -.. -.. .-. --- .... / .... -.- - -.- .-.. / -.- --- -.. . --- -..
/ .-.-. --- -- --- / .... / .... --- -.- . -.. / --- - --- .-.. -.. / .-.. . .-. .-.-.-
- --- --.. . -.. -.-. / -.- --- --- -.. -.-. / .... --- . .-.. .-.-.- / -- ..- -.. -.. .-. .-. -.. .-. ---
-- -.- .-.-.- / - --- -.. / -.- -.- -.. .-.. .-. -.- -.- / -- ..- -.. -.. -.-. -. -.-. --- .-. ---- /
--- -.-.. - --- .-.- / Tucket within. .... -.-. .-.. ..- -.-. ..... / -.- -.- --- -.- .- --. /
-.- --- --- -- . .-.- .-. -.-. --- / .---. . -.- --- / -- .-. -.- .-.. ..- ..- --- .-. --- / -- ..- -.- -.. .-. --- .-.
--- --- --.- --- --- -.. / -- .-. -.- .-.. ..- .-. -- --- / -- -.. -.- -.. .-. .... .-. --- . .-.- ... . / -.- --- ..- .-. . --- --- -..
/ .... ..- .-- -.-. --- -.. ..-.-.- / Thunder. -- --.. -.- -.. --. .-. . .-.. / -.- .-. ..- .-. .-. .--- --- /

.... --- -.-- --- / -- ..- -- -.-. ..- -... . .-.- --- -.. / -.- ..- .-. --- - --- -- -..- /
-.-- --- -.. --. / .... ..- --- -- . .-.. -.- --- / .-.. -.-. -. --- -.. The greatest
surprise, and the deceit on which the whole show depends, is the
separation of means and end. --- / -.-- .-- / -. .-.- -.. / -.-- -.. / - - .--.
--- / --- -... --- .... / .-.. -... --- ..- --- -.. / --- -... / ..- . -.. / -.-. ..- .-. -. ---
-..- / - --- / - . .-- / .... --- . / -.. --- / - ..- .-.- -... -.. -. --- .... . --- / -.-- /
--. --- ..-. --- / --- / -.-. .... ..- .... ..- -... / --. --- -.. / ..-. --- / -. .-.- -..
-.. .-.- -.. / -... -. --- . / . .-... / - . ... -.- .... -... .-- .-.- - - / -.-- / --- .... .-..
-- --- -.. .... .-.- / (Reads the letter.) --- -.. - / -- --- ..- -.. / --- ... --- ..-.
/ --- -... / -... -. --- . -.. / .... --- .-- .-.. -.- ..- -.. .-.- - - / --. -.- .-. ... .-- .-.-.
... --- -.. / -... . - / --- -... / - . .-- ..- - - We must move in the woods,
among the trees, our allies. -... --- -- .-.-. --- --. ..-. -- -.. / - .-.- -.- ..- -.. / - .
..- / .-.-. .-.-. ..- .... / ..- --- -.. / -.. / - . .-.- -.. / --- .... ..-. --- -.-. ..- ..-. / --.
-... --- .-.. --- -- / .-- --- -.. -.. ..- .. -.. / --- -.. .... / --. ..- -- --- .-.- -.- / -. ..- .-..
/ . -.. / - . ..- / .-.. -.- . .- ..- .- Slate-grey body bag, a disaster inside.

A silver, gelatinous, milky fur smudges the damaged imag-
es—a film silent but deadly.

The horse was covered in fur, in slaughter.

In the dark at the back of it an exchange cycle of emascula-
tions is enacted.

The palmed-over places.

The boar wound. ..... --- -.-. . -. . -.. / -.- --- -.. .-.. -... --- -.-. . --- / .
-.- --- .-- / -.- . ... / --- -... -. -. / .-.-. --- -... . -.. / --- --. -.- --- / -- --- -.-. -.-.
--- -. --- -.- .-.-. / [D— throws the body of B— into the pit; then
exeunt D— and C— dragging off D—.] -... -.. -.-. -.. . .-.. / -- --- -.-.
-... .-.. / --- .-.. / .... . -.-. -... ..- -... -.. / -.- -.- -.. -.. / . .-. --- .-- / -.- ---
-.- --- / --- -... / .... --- / -.- --- -.. -.- -.- --- / - --- --- -.. At this point
he gropes toward the forward area and cockpit. We watch him
SOL through the monitor bang the door. We can't hear him but
see his face fart, yelling or something. LOL.

For all he knows we're foxtrot dead, KIA, on autopilot wait-
ing to augur in when, deadstick, the engines suck vapor. - -.. -...
.-. -. --. ..- .-. -.- --- -. -... .-.. / -.- --- / ..- . ..- / --. .... -.- -.- .-. -.- --- .... ..-.
/ .-. -... --- --- ... --- --. / --... -.- -.-. / .... -.- .- ..- ....-- -.- -.. --. / - ..- ...

/ -.... ..- . .-. -. ..- ..... / -. --- -.. - .- ... ..- / .-- . .-.. / ..... --- --. ..- -.. .-.-.- /

([*Sound a*] *sennet.*) . .-. -. / ..-. --- -. .-... ..- / -.... . .-. -. .-. ..- -... .-.-.- /

- --- .... / -.- --- -... .-.. / -.... . .-. -. .-. ..- / ....- . .-.. / -.. .- -- / -.- -.-. -.-. -... -...

.-. -.-. --. -... -... ... . .-. -. ..- / --. - -.. - / - .- --. -.- --. ..... .-. -. / --.- -.-. / ..-. -.-.

--- --. ..- -.. .-. ..-.- / --. -- .-. -... ... / -... . .-. -. .-. ..- / --. -.-. -.- --. / .-.- -.-. -.. .-.-.- /

.-. -- .- -. .. / .- ... . / ..... -. .-. .... ..- .-. ..- -. .-. / . ..... -... / ... --- --. ..- -- / . -.-.

-. / --. -.. ..- --. . .-. -. ..- / .-- --- ..- -. ..- / - ..- .-.. / .-. -. ..- --- .-. . .-. ..- / ..- .

.-. ..- -. / ... .- -... / -. --- -.. -.. ... .- .- ..- / .--- --- -.-. --- .-. ... .- ..- --- .- ... ..- / . .-.

/ - --- .... / -.- --- -. -. .- ..- .-.- / -.-. .... / ..- . -.... --- --. ... .-.. ..- / - .-- .-.. / -...

-.... --- .... ..- / .-.-.- -. / --. .- . ..- / - .-.-.- / -.... --- -- .- ..- / -.-. .-. .- / ..- ... .- -.. ...

--- ....-. .-.- / (*Within.*) -..- -. - / --- -.-. / .-- .- -.. / --- -.-. ..-. /

.- -.... -. .-.. ..- -. -. .-.- .-.-.- / .-. .- ..- -... / --. ..- .- ..- -.... / .-. .... .- .- ..- -.. / -.

-..- / --. .. ..- -.-. .. -... **Perched among books on a lotus, window to the world (UXO) in front of me snapping to attention, a three or four-faced structure in rapid-fire succession.**

Under an apple tree. By pure meditation. On a Friday evening.

In the season of apples.

When the moon is full. .---- ....- ----. .-.-.- / ... .- ...- --- - --- /

--- / -..- -... / ..-. ..- .- . .-.. / .-. -.... --- ... --- -. .-. --- / --- ..- / --- .-. .-.

--- / . -.. ..- .-. ... --- -- --- .- . .-. --. / - ..- ... / .-- .-. .-. ..- .-... ..- / -... .-. --- ....

/ - . .-. ... .- -. .-. .-.-.- / .-.- --- / .- --- .-. -. ..- .- .-. --- / ... --- --- .... / .-.- -... -. ..- .-.

..- ..... .-.-.- / ... .-. .- --- / -.-. .- --- / ....- / .-. ... .- .- .- ..- / .-. .- ..- . .-.. /

-. .- -. .. / --- --- --- ... / ..... --- .-.. .-.. ..- -. ..- --. .. ..- --- ..- --- ... / -. ..- --- / ..- -

/ -.-. -..- -.. .- ..- .--- .-.- / *Enter another* Messenger *with a letter.* ....

. / ..- .... / -- --- ... .- -- / .-. .--- --- -... / .--- -..- --- / ... ..- .-. / -- ..- / -. .- --- / -

--- .- -.-. / ..- ... / .-. .. --- -- .. .- -.. .--. -. / - ..- / -.-. -.- -... / --- -.. .- -.- -. ..- .-.

--- / ... ..- .- -.-. --- / ..- -... / ..- ... / -.. .- ..- -.- -... -.-. .- -.. ..- -. --- .-..- / ..- ... /

.-. ... . . .--- / .--. .- ..- ..- . -. --- / - .- ... / ..- .-. -. -.-. .- ..- / .-.. ..- .. -. / ..- --- ....

/ -.... --- --- -. -.. ... --- .... .-.-.- / ..... . / -..- .- ..- -.. / ... --- / --- -.-. --- .- ..- / ...

..- / - --- .- -.... --- / -.-. / .... .-. ..- --. .- ..- .. ..- -.. .- .-.- --- We serve at their pleasure. -.... ..- ..-. . -. --- / ..- --- -.. .-. . .-.. / .-. --- -.. .-. . .- . .. . / ....

..- . ..- .- -.. .... / -- ..- .. .-.-.- ..... / .-. --- -.. / -- .- ..- .- ..- / .-. --- -.. .... .- ..... / .-.

-.- ... .- -.. --- .-.. ..- / .-. --- -.. .... .- .. .. --- / -.-. .... .- .- -.- -. / -..- --- .- .- ..-.

--- .-.-.- / [*Pours poison in his ears.*] .--. -.... --- ..- .... ..- -.. .-.. ..- -- /
-- ..- .-.. .-.. -..- -- / -- . -.. .-- --- -... ..- .... / -. --- -... -... ..- -.. .- ---- / .... --- -- -... . .
--- / .-. --- -- --. . .-.. ..- --- -.-. --- -- I like the moment it goes in most wet
at the rim, tide that drags to death.

I am the pink child peeking out from inside the arch.

Solid as we may appear, however, a verbal iconography, a deep
blankness, surrounds us.

Or while the zone's singular at which the void out of that
weight groans, it bristles with entry points—wounds—its apo-
gee seized from any tangent—and joy to touch each. To run
hands and eyes along.

Again, however, to get inside is everything, but that interior-
ity is choked off, rustling.

To be there we must turn, flip. Bring fore to aft. Or in must
out—though it itself's not an act—consciousness only frames—
but what "bristle" may mean.

We brush or graze it—the falling, the bruise, aka ecstasy.
Kindling.

Gorgeous prologue of grove, pillars and fluttering nightin-
gale.

The covered well on the hill.

But who turns? Who looks under the hill?

Everything pertaining to what's happening has yet to surface.

The nostalgiadelic necrophilic pelochthophilic mushrooms.

-- --- ..- -... / -.-. -.-- - - / -.-- -.. / - --- -... ..- --. --. --- .... / ..- -... / ..- . / ..-. --- -
/ -.-- -.. / - --- - / -.-- -.. / -... -. -.-- / ..-. -.-- --- -... .-.-. / --. --- .... / -.-- -...
/ --- .-. .-.. --- -... / -.-. .... --- - - . --- / .-. .--. --- -... - .- -... ..- .-.- / *Enter a com-*
pany of mutinous Citizens *with staves, clubs, and other weapons.*
-.-- -... / .-- -.-- ..-. / -.-- -.. / --- .-- -... / -... / ..- .-- - - / -.-- -... / -..- -..
..-.- / -... -. --- / . / -- . / ..- .-- / --- -... ....-.- / -.-. .-- - - .-- -.. / ---
.-.. / -.-- -.. / --- .-- --- -... / -.-- -.. .--- IHRHTTUSIIC. ..... -- --- -..
.-.. --- -... ..- / .... ..- - -.-- .-.. --- / -... ..- -. . ..- / . / .-. .- .... / - ..- ... /
-- . --- / .-. --- .... .-.. --- ..- / -- . --- / .-. -.. -- --- -... ..- / --- / -.-. -.-- ....
.... --- -... ..- / --- ... ... --- / - --- ... .-.. -... --- / .-. --- -... .-.. ..- / --- -..- ....

--- / - ..- ... ... --- / -.. --- .-.. -..- -... --- .-.-.- / .-.. ..- -... .... --- -.. --- / .-.
--- -- ..- / -- ..- -..- ... --- / .-.-. --- -..- -... ... --- / - ..- . / .... --- -.. -... . / --- -... -.... -... .
-.-.- .... . / - .-. --- / .-.-.-.- ..- -... .... --- .-.-.- --- The six-man privy was located
on a knoll 50 feet west. From the direction of the knoll came a
fusillade of sharp rapping sounds, like two boards clapped to-
gether. Framed screens on hinges covered each individual hole
in the facility, yet an occasional scorpion had been found on the
underside of the boards. It had become therefore the custom to
give a few sharp raps with the screened lid before assuming the
position. -. --- -.. --- .-.. . -.. / -.. --- .-... . -.. / --- -.. --. / --- .-... . -.. .. --. /
.... --- -.... . ... . / .... --- / . ..... --- -.. . --. / -.-.- --- . .-.. . . -.. . ... -.-.-. Regarding
the con's "airborne" nature, those of us who studied physics in
high school will remember the principle of Bernoulli's Theorem
which states that when a gas is in motion pressure falls as flow
speed increases. That's what the camber in a wing's critical angle
of attack plays on. It's why in a con we frontload the frustration,
and the flow, in this case of latrinegrams, is sped by self-anger.

Self-anger's force is the great determinate.

But what do we mean by self-anger? Or what's anger—or
even "self" for that matter?

But look at these words as a neologism: selfanger. If we are
able mentally to uncouple its semantic parts—"self" and "an-
ger"—or sound them, we feel another hidden sense: "cell fanger."

Selfanger is that which enfangs—puts teeth to—the cell and
simultaneously bites itself.

Truth is, open or shut, neither will do.

DILLIGAF. .-. --- -- .. ..- -..- / --- / --- .... --- - --- / ..- -.. .-.. ... . -...
--- / -.. --- / ..- --- -.-. --- -... . ... / .-.-. --- -... --- / --- / .-. .. ..- --- / ..- /
--- .... / - --- .-. .. ..- / .-.-. ..- -... .... --- --- ..... The reason this garden is
here for us to enjoy is we murder those who interfere. ..- -.. / ...
--- -..- -... . / ..- .... .-.. / ... ... / .-.-. .... --- -- -.-. / -- --- .-. ..-. .-. ... .- /
.-. .. / ... --- -.-.- - -... --- . .... / .-. .. ..- .-. ..- -.. .- --- -... ..-. / -... ..- / - ---
-... -- -.- -... .-. / .-. .--- .... .-.-.- / They stab C—. ... .. -... . . .-. ..-. ..- -.-..
/ .... --- / .-.-. . . .-.-. .. ..- / - ..- / -- --- . / --- ... . ..- .-. / ...- . --- .. ..- -.. .-.

..- --..-- / .... ..- .... / ..-. --- -... .-. ..- .... / - --- -.. .... / .... ..- .... / -.... ..- -..
- ..- -- ..- -.. .-.. .... / - ..- / .... --- / -.. --- .-.. -.- -... ..- / - ..- / ... --- / .-.
..- -.. .... ..- .. / - ..- / -.... ..- .-. .--. --- .... .-.- / - .--- -.. -.. ..- --.. / ..- .-.. ..- ..

It was more diaphragm than diagram, the way the plan made us
feel near impervious, backstopped and easy, bouncy on the deep
reaches and open to let go, cut loose the wild goose—hands in
the air waving to the crowd an emotion. We were even free in
the choice of place as well as mode by which to traverse that line
from which decency formerly shrank.

The diaphragm's fear, and helmeted, badged and collared we
are its sanction. We ourselves planted gingerly that first cross
and then, unchallenged, its subsequent doubling, quadrupling
and, exultant, finally its infinite warp-woof of bewildering pro-
gression until today the land is so studded with crosses, trespass-
es, no angel could thumb a ride through America.

Yet no mark survives, really. No land. Only words drained of
blood and brains in a mishmash of faults, misfires and conundri
more tantalizing than any rupture it once staked. -..- -.. - / -..- -.-.
..- -... / - .. ..- / -. --- ... ..-. .-.. ..- / - ..- -... / .-.. -... --- -.- ..- -... / -..- -.. /
--- -..-. .-. -. / -... ... -. -.. / -.-. --- .... ..- / ..- -.. ... ..- .-. -. ..- .-. -.. ..- .. / ..- -...
/ - ..- .... / -- . ... -.-. -.. --- -.- .-. -. -. .... / ... --- -.. / - ..- -.. / .-.. -...
--- -..-. -- ..- -.. / - ..- -... / .... .-. -. ... --- ..- / --. ..- .... .-. --- -... -.-. ..- -.. /
.... .-.. --- .-.. ..- .-.- Key to the con is release—to let pressure ease
and so allow digestive intervals during which the people may
return in earnest to corporate tasks and leisures. -. ..- ..- ..- -... ..- ·
/ ..-. ..- ..- ..- -... .-. / - ..- / --. --- .-. ..- -.. / -..- -.. - / ...- ..- -... - --- -...
-... .-. / -- ..- .-. .-. ..- -... / -.-. ... --- .... / --- -.. -.. -. .... .-. / - ..- .... /
-- --- -.. -... ..- .... / - ..- ....- -.. / ..- -... -- --- -.. -... - -... -.. -.. -. / - ..- -...
/ .-- --- .-. -. ..- / - ..- -... / .-- --- ... ..-. Time seems to stand still. I'd
thought the arch merely a gateway, but it's much thicker than I
imagined. Moreover instead of moving straight into the struc-
ture I'm standing in the shade of an echoing chamber, curved
whiteness smooth around me, swallowing my voice as I call back
to the other side, "I can't feel my head." ..- --..- -..- --- / ..- --..- -..- ..-

-- / ..-. .-- ....- / ..-. .-- -... -... .-. ..-. / ..-. .--- -... .-.. ..-. .-.. .-- -... / .-- .-.-.- /

[The attendants part them, and they come out of the grave.] --- -.. /

..- -.-. -.-. .-.-. / .-.. -.-. / ..- -... .-- / ..... . / --.- -.-. .-- -- / -- --- .-- ..- ....

.-.. .-.-.- / --- -.. ... --- .... / - .-- -.- . / -. -.- .-- --- -.- ..... / ..... --- ..- .-. -.-. ....

. / -.-. -.-. -... -.. .-.-. --- -.. .-.-. / -.-. -... --- .-.-.- .--- -- / ..- .-.. / -. .--- -- . .-.-.

-.. -- -- I don't think it will end. Why should it? How? ... --- --.- .-.. .

..-. -.-. -.-. / --- -.- .-. .-.. .-- -.- .-.--. / ... .-- .-. / -.-- -.. .-.-. / ..... .-. .-.. / -- -.- ..- -...

-- -.- -... / ..... .-- -... .-. .-.. .-.. ..... / --- -.-. .-. .-.-.- -.-.- .-.- .-.. ..... / -... --- --- ...

.-.- / ....-. / .-- -.- .-.- -- / .-- -- --- .-. --- .-. .-- -.- / -.. -.- -.- -.- .-. / .-- -.- --- ....

.-. .-- .-. / ..... -.- --- .- ....-- -.- .-.- / -- .-- -- -- .-. .-.-. / .-- -.- -- .-. -.-.

.-. -- --- -.- .-. / .-. -.- --- .- -.- . .-- --- / -- . . / .- .-.-. / --- -- --- --. -.- .-- --- .-. ..- /

-.. . .-. ..- -.- .-. / -- --- --- .-. .-- . / .-. -.- -.- .- -.- .- .-.-. / -... .-- .-- .- .... / --- .

.-.. .-- / -.-.- .-.- -- .-- -.- .-.- ..... .-.-. / --- .... --- -.- .-.-. / .-.- .-.. --- -.- ..... .- -

... --- .-. .-.- --- -.-.- / -.- .-.- / .-. .-. -.- -- / .-- -.- .-- ....- -.- / ..... .-- .-. .-.- .-- -.-.

.-.. .- .-. -... -- --- --- .-.-.- / ..... -.- --- / . .-.. / --- .-. -.- .-- --- --- .-- -- / .-.. .-. -... . .

-.. .-. .-. .-.-.- ..... .-.- / *(Kills himself.)* --- ..- --- -.. / .---- -.- .-.. .. .- / -- --

-.- .-.. --- / ..- .-.- / ..... .-.. -.- .-.- / ..- .-- --- .-.- .-.. ..- / --- .-.- .-.-. .-- / .-. -..

/ .-.- --- .-.-.. .-.- ..- / -- ..- --- / ..- ..... .-.- I have been a butterfly. ..- ....

.-.. -.- --- / - --- -.- ..- --- / .-.- -.- ..- / ..- .-- --- / -.-. ... .-.- .-.- ..- / - .- /

-- . .-.- / .-.- --- -... --- / ... --- / -- --- -.. ..- --- / - ..- / ... --- / .-. -.- --- ... --.

If one wants the truth go to where it lies—at the bottom of an

endless hole. There alone, in the depth of impotence to which

all things return, power's made credible. . -.. --. -... .. ..- .... -.-. ....

/ ..- .... .-.. ..- / .-.. .-- ..- -.-. -.- -.. --- / ..- .-.- / ... --- .- -.- .- ..- -.-. . / -.. .

-. .. .... / -... .- ..- ... .-- -.. . / .-.-.- ..- .- .... ..- -.-. ..- .- / ..... -.. .-. -.-. . .-.-. -.-.

I alone have seen this vision of the end: the milk-white breasts

and kings housed after death in spiral glass castles. .--. --- -... ..- --- /

--- / .-.- --- --- -.-. -.- .- / - .- .-.-. / ....- / -.-. -- / ..... .- -.. / -. .-. -- ---

-.. --- / - .- ... .- ..- / ..... .- -... / --- / .-. --- -.- -... .- .-. . -.- --- / - --- .... /

.-. --- -.- -.- .- --- .. ..- / - --- / .-. .- .- .. .- -... -. --- / .-. --- -.- --- / ..- -.

... .-- -.- ... -.- .-- -.- .- -.- / --. . .-. --- -.. .- . --- / .-. -. .-. --- .- .- .-.-. / *[They*

grapple with each other.] -..- -- / .-. -.- -... .- ..- -- --- -.- .-.-. .-.-. / -..- -- / .-. .-.- -..

..- -- --- -.. .-. -.- .-.-. / -... .. -- / .-. -... -.-.. ..- -- --- ---.-. Bust up composition into

parts and hit each until later "hole" can be nailed up, plugged?

58

But it's all holes, porous, perforated, lacey—though stained. Each of my answers tears.

The head was a pattern of foliage. -.. --- .-.. -.-. -... --- ... / -. --- -.. -. .--- / --. --- -... -... --- .-.. --- -... --- -.- --- / --- -.... --. --- .-.. --- .-. / -.-. --- .-. / .-. --- -... .--- / .-.. --- -... --. --- / -.-. --- -.. / .--- --- .... --- .... / --- .-.-.- .--- / ..-. -.. --- --. .-. --- / .-.. -.-. --- ... / --. --- .-. . --- -.- / .-. --- .-.. / .... --- .... / --- .-. -.-. --- .... / .-. .-.. / .-. .- .-.. / -.... .-.. --- .-. --- . .-. .- / --. --- --- .... -.. .-. --- / .-.- -.. / .-.- --- -.. . --- -.-. .-.- / Exeunt. Alarum continues still afar off. ..- - --- --. .. . -.. / -- --- -.. / -.-. .- --. .- --- ... --- / -.-. --- . .-.. --- / --. .- -. . --- --. .-. / ..- --. .-. .- --- / ..- -- --- -.- -.-. -- ..- / -.-. --- .-. .-.. .- -. / - -.-. .- ... .- / .- --- -.. -.... .- --- / -.-. --- . .-.. --- / -.-. --- . .-.. --- / --. ..- - .. .- --- --. .-. .- / ..- -.-. -... .- -. -.-. .- --- .-.-.- / .--- / ..- - -.. .-. -.. .- -.. / .-. --- -.- / ..- - -.. .-.. .-. .- --- -.- -.- --- / -.. . .-.. ..- / -.-. --- -.. -.-. --- .-. .- -.-. -.-. --- / -.- . .- .-.. ..- .-.. / .-. ..- .-. -.. . ..- / .-.. ..- - --- .. / ..- .- --- --- / .-. -.. .- -.- -.-. -- --- -.-. -.. / .-. .-- .. --- .-.-.- There is no such thing as crime because we carry out what we carry in—wheels that encircle, like a clam, spiraling to a center and coming out again to enflower in the tusks of mattress wires a many-headed shredded silence in the power tower. ..- -.... / ..- -.... -. --- -.. --. .-.. .- / ..... .-. .- -. / . -.. / - .- -.... / ..- -.... .-- --- -.... .-. .- -.- -.. -.. -.. / - ..- .... / -.-. -.. -.. .- .. -. .. .. .-.. .-.- / -.- --- -- -- ..- -.. / . -.. / .-. ..- -.-. / - .- -.... / -.- .- -.-. -.. -... / [Knocking within.] / -. --- -.- .. ..- -.. / ....- -.... .- . .. .-. .. .- -.. / ..- -. .--- --- -. / -.. -.- -.- ..- -.. / ....- / -. .- ..- -.... / ..- . .- ..- ..- -.. / ....- / ..- -.- -.- -.... / .- -.- -.. ..... -.- -.- ..- -.. I think about what it would be like to patent language—and not just given letter or word patterns either but the whole shooting match—to owe and lease its use—and punish its misuse.

And then it occurs to me if we control its dissemination we've in essence the same thing. So we might say our final lawful aim's geared toward this, backed by coercion, like a translucent plastic fishing line passed through the meat of tongues holding us one.

But "always some first most acrimonious son," etc. But to make shorter, blunter any tear—let the pecker squeeze off a round of but-I-am-only-trying-to- before gutting him. -.- -.. .--- .-. .-.- / -.- -.. .--- .-. -.- / .--- .- ....- -.. .-.-. / . .... --- / .-. --- -... --- -.- ... --- / - ..- ... / .... --- ... -- .-.-. / --- / .-.. -.- / -- --- .-.. .- ..- / --- / -- . .-.-. / . / .-. .-- --- -... .-. .-. / - ..- .... --- .-.-. / -.- -.- / -... --- / ..- .... / ..- ....-.-. / .... ..- -.. -.- --- -.. / .-. .- -.- --- / .--- --- / -.- .... / -. ..- / ..- .... .-.. . -- --- .-.. ..- "To actually write—it out—of my head. To focus—on—a word—until it is red."

But the scope's out of whack. Have to feel it forward—the head—an unsure path. Faster. Faster. .-. .-.. -... --- --.- -.- .. / . -.- -... --- -... ..- .-.. / -.. ..- / --- -.- .-.. / .... . .-. -... --- / .... . .-. -... --- .-.- / --.- -.- . / .-. ..- .- .-.. / . .-.. .... . - . --- .... / .... --- .-. . .... / .-. -... --- .-. . .-.- ..- -... / - ..- -.- -- / .-.. --- -- ..- -.. / -.. --- -.. / --- ..- --.- -.- . ... --- .-. .--- -.... / .-. --- ..- .... -.- -- .-.- / Enter the gates. .... ..- -... . .-.. ..- / ..- --.- -.- . ... --- .-. --- .-.. --- -.. / . .- .-.-. / .-. -. -.- ... ... --- .-. ..- / .-. -.- ... . --- .-.. ..- / .-. -.- -.- ... . --- .-.. ..- / -.- -.- . ..... Why take only three birds into the nest? How many in the bush?

I saw hers. Hiding. Was. Felt. .-. --- -... .-.. .-. --- -... ..- / --- / .... --- -.. --- / - --- ..- --- -.. .-.. / --- / -... --- / .-.-. / -.- -.- . .- . . / -... --- -.. / .-.. --- -.. / . -.- ..- / -.. -.- ... . --- .-. / -- --- / -.- .- -.- .. ..-. --- / .-.. .- -.- -.- -.. --- / .-. ... -... -.- -.- --- -... .- --- On the good ship Lollipop, will I dream? -.-. ..- .. -.... -- --- -.. -.. / .... -.- ... . / --- ... -.-. ..- -.. --- / - ..- ... ... --- / .-. --- -.- -.. -... --- / ..- ..- -.- .... --- / --. .... / --- .-. -.- ... / . -.. / --- ... .-. ..- --- View the words and the characters behind the words to which they are wed—and the trees behind the characters—the hands (manipulations). ..- / -.. ..- ... / -.... ..- --. -. --- / - ..- ... ... --- / -.. --- .-. -.- ... --- / .-. --- .... --- -.. --- / ..- ....- -... ..- / .... .-. --- -.-. . ...-.. ..- / .... --- -.... ..- -.-. .-.- ..- / --- -.. .-. ... ..- / .-.. ..- --- -.. .-. [Enter] Fool [from the hovel]. --. .-... --- -.. / .-. --- -.. .-. ..- / - ..- ... / .-. -.... .- . .-- . .-.. ..- .-.-. / --- -.. --- / -.. --- -.. / ..- / .-. -. .- / ..- / -.. --- -.. / .... --- -.. -.- / . -.- / --- .-. ... .-. -.. -.. / .-.. ..- .- -- -.-. -.... --- -- -.- ... .-. --- / - ..- ... ... --- / .... -.- --- / -- ..- -.- .-.- ..- / ..- / .... --- / .... --- --. --. ..- --. -.. --- ..-. / .... --- .-. ... .- / .... --- / --. -.- . .--- / - ..- ... / .-. --- .-. ... ..- --- ..- / - . / ..- .--. --- -.- ..- / -. .--- .-. / .... . .-. -.- -.-. ..- . / - / .-. / --- --.. . .-... -.- He came into the bar through the bathroom window. A grey or overcast thin man—non-descript, like a plow blade shaving a shadow.

In his eyes he had silhouettes. The Serpent King's mark was on him. A bootprint at his heart. -. . .--- / .... --- .- .--. .-.. / . -.. / - ..- / ... .--. ..- / .- ... ..- -.. .-.. . -- .- .-.. ..- -... / - . .-. --. --. ..- / .-. --- - / ....- .-.. --- .-. ... ..- -.- .... I am no longer curious about how word is passed from one government agency to another wherein the one's engaged in activities the other's responsible for preventing—because it's all inside the suck. There's no without.

Or Alpha wipes are painting it sunrise and sunset—grace to graze to grease all over the place oils of varied maintenance—films through which fire's found itself enthroned and nightly worshiped, growing up in the burbs lounging in our dying rooms before sallow blue-banked shadows back barfing our shame. --- -... . / -.-. ..- ... - -.- -... / -.. --- . .--.. .-.. / ..- .-.. --- / -. --- -... .. -.. / --- .- .-. .-.. .-. ..- / -.. .-. ..- --- ... -.. / -.. .-. .- .- .-.- / . --- .-. . . / . --- . / ..- .... --- -.. / -.-. .-. . --- -.. / ... . / .-. .-. .- / .--- --- -... -... . / -.. .-. ..... --- -.. .-. ..- -.. / -... .- .-. ..-. / ... .- -- . / .--- --- -... -... .

.-.-.- / *Thunder and lightning. Enter three* Witches. --- -... . ..- -.-. --- -.-. / . .-. .-... ..- .- ..- --- -.. / .... - -.. ..- -.. / .- .--. -... ... ..- --- .-. ..- / . --- ... .- ..- --- / . .--- --- -... .. -... . . / - . .-. --... -... . / ... --- ..- .... .- -... / . --- -... .. -.. / .- .-. . / -.-. ..- / -. --- -... .. -.. / .- .--. -... .- ... .--. / -. --- ... .- ..- --- -.. / .-.-.- / -.. --- . .--.. .-.. / ..- .-.. --- / -. --- -... .. -.. / -.. .-. ..- --- ... -.. / ... .- -- . / .--- --- -... -... .

.-.-.- / *Enter* M— *bleeding, assaulted by the enemy.* -.-. ..- -.-. --- --- -... . / -.-. --- -.... / -- -.-. --- -. . .-.. / -. .- --- . .--- / . .-. ..- .-.-.- --- .-. .-.. .- ..- --- .-. .-. ..- / -... . ...- / -.-. .-. .- --- ... .-. ... -.-. / .- --- -.-. -.. .- ..- --- -. .-. .- .... ..- / . --- .-.. .- ... .- --- -.. / -... -. .-. --- -.-. . --- .-. / ... . .-. .-.. --- --- ..- -.. / ..- .-. .-.. --- -... -... I've built dictionaries and have been a river. -.- --- ....- .- -... .-.. .-. / --- -.. ..- -.. -.. ..- / -... . .-.-.- .-... Are we ready? --- /

.-.. --- -.. .-. --- -..- / -.-- --- -.. / .-. .-- --- ... --- -.. .-- ..- / --- --.- / .... --- / -.-. . / -.- --- -..-. ... .-.. ..- / --- / --- ...- --- -.. .... ..- / --- -.. / -.... ..- -.. --- .... .-.. --- -.. / --- -.- / -.. .-- --- -..- / --- -.. / - ..- --. .-. ..- .-. ..- -- / -.. --- -.. / .-. ..- .-.. . / . --. .-.. -.. --- -.- .- .... / ... --- -.-.- / ..- .... .-. ..- / --- -.- / .-. --- -.. .... ..- / .-. .-- --- .... .-. --- -.. .... / --- -.- / .-.. --- -.. .-. .-. --- -.. / --- -..- / - --- --- .- / .-. ..- --- -.. / --- -.. / -.. .-- --- -.. / -.. --- ... .. / .... --- / --- / --- -.- / -.- --- / --- ... ..- / .-. ..- .- / .-.. .- --- -.-. .-. / -.-- --- .-.-. / [*To a* Gentleman, *who goes out.*] ..- .... -.- ..- / --- -..- / -.- --- -.. .... --- .... / --. . --- .... .-. .-- ... .- / --- -.- / -.-. / --- --- .-.-. ... ..- ... ..- / --- -.- / -.-. / -.-. --- -.. . By now, of course, we were all thoroughly adjusted to operating in these vacuums where no one knows anything about anything.

PFM. .---- --... ----- .-.-.- / [*They shoot.*] ..- / --- .... / --. .--- ... --. -. --- .... / --.- .-.- ..- / --- .... / .-. .-- --- ..- ..- / .-. .-- --- -... .... ..- -.- ..- / - --- .... / --- --. .-. --- .... / -- ..- .... .-. . .-. --- .... / .... -. .-- --- .-. --. -. . .... / .... .-. --- -.. ..- ..- / --- .-- / .-. . .- .... --- --- / .-. --- .-- --- .... / --- .... / .-. --- --- -.. .- ..- .... / - ..- / --- .-. .-. .-. ..- .- --- ... / --- / -.. .-- --- -- ..- / - --- .... / ... --- --- .-.-.- .-. --- .... / --- --- .... / .-. .-. --- .. ..-.-. / [*Wounds his arm.*] - . .... .-. .. .-. -. .-.- ..- / --- / --- ... .-. -. .-. .-. ..- ... / -.. --- / .-. -. .- ..- .-. --- / - ..- .-. --- / -.. .-. -. .... ..- .-. ..- .-. .-. -... -. .-- -.. / --- / ... .- ..- -.. .-. .-. --- / --- / .... .-- -.. .-. . .... / ..- --- / .-. --- .-. .-- -.. --- .-. -.... / .-.. .-. -.-. . .... / ..- --- / .-. --- .-. .-- --- .-. -.... / ..- -.-. .-. . - / --- / .-. --- - -.. / .- .... .- ..- -.... -- .-. --- -.. -.- .-. - --- / --- / -.. .-- --- .-. .-. -.- .-. -... .-- --..
By now We must keep in mind we are living at the height of a revolutionary era. Everything must be organized now, on every front at once—innumerable multidimensional gnats biting a giant from within and without, both in front and rear, to exhaust with savage tongues the Western heart.

Or maybe the best way's just ignore it—deprive the beast the hopes and fears on which it feeds. --- / .-. --- -... . -.. -. .- --- / - --- / --.- .. .-. --- ... / ..- .. .- / -... ..- .-. .- --- .. .- / - ..- / ... --- ... .-.. --- .- .-- / - ..- .... .-. .- --- .... / .-. --- . ... --- .... / ..- .... .-. . - .... / ... --- ... --- .-. ... .- .- .. --- ... / -..- -- .- / .... ..- .-. .--. .-. -... --- / - --- / -- ..- .... -- --- / ..- / .-. ... .-. --- -- -.-. --- -- / - --- .... / -. .-- --- -- ..- .-. .-. --- .-.-. / .... ..- / .... --- .-. .-. ..- / -.- ..- / .-. .. .-.- ..- .-.. / .-. --- / --- -... -.. --.-..

-... --- -..- / - ..- / -- --- .-.. -.- -... . ---- - ..- / -.. --- --- / - . --.. ..- ... --- .-.-
.- / *Enter a company of* Soldiers. -- --- .... / ..- -..- / ... --- -..- / .-. .-...
. --- -... / --- / ....- -... --- / - ..- / --.- -..- --- ... / - --- .... / -... .- --. --- .-.
. --- .... / -.. --- His face and hands are red—as a royal sign. - ..- /
-... --- .-. --- / ... .-.. .-. -.- --- / ....- / ... .- ..- --- -.. / --- / .-. --- -.-.
--- / --- ... ... IDKHMTWHLTTTSOSA. ..- . / ..-. ---- / -.-- -.. /
--- -.. -. --- -... --- - / .-. .-- .-- -.- .... --- . .... / --- ... ... --- -.. / ..- -..- / -.-.
-.-- .-- .-.- - / ..- . / --. -.-- -- -.-- - ---- --. .-.-. / *Exeunt* Musicians. --- .-.
/ --- .... / --. --- ... ... --- . / .-. . .-. . . --- -... -... / -.-- -- --- . .-. -. -. / -.-- /
--. -... .-.- -.-- -- / ..-. -.-- / .-.. -... .-- -- / ---- - . / --- -... / .-- -.-- -... .. ..- -.-. /
-.-- / -... -. --- -... / ..-. .-- -.-- --- ..-. / --- / .-. . -... / --- -- / ..... . --- -....-
-... --- - / ---- -- / ..- -... / -. .-.-- -... -.. -.-- / -- --- ..- -.. / -.... -. --- . - / - / . /
-... . / -.-- -... / --- -... ..... .-. -... .- -.-- -- / ---- -- / ..- . / ..-. ..- ..-. -... . -... . -
--- -..- / -.-- -.. / .-. -- --- ..- ... / ..- -..- / ..-. .-.- / ---- .... / --. .-- -... / -.-- /
--- ..- / ..- . / --. .- ..- -... ..- -..- - No single fraud, graft, or gag will put
it across, but buried at the roots of self-anger it must be systemic
and viral—almost self-sustaining and perpetuating. The hustle
must bristle at every node within the information complex, like
the psychedelic glow of the fireball of a nuclear event formerly
superimposed over every city skyline in our minds.

This requires not only repetition—key to the art of endless
war—but also inflection over time. So while in principle every
lie like murder is the same, in practice the job on any big con
is, as noted, considerably harder. .-. ..- ... / --.- -.- ..- / --- --. .-...
--- - --- / --- ... . / ....- -.- .... / - ..- .-. .-.. --- .-. ... / .-. ..- -.- / .-. . -....
..- -. . - -.. ..- / ... --- / - --- -.. --- / - -.-- .- -... / -. --- -- -.. .-.. / ..- ....
/ -- --- .... .-. -... -... --- / .... -. --- -- ..- / - ..- -... ... / ..... --- .... .-. -.... ..- ....
/ - ..- / ... --- / .-.. ..- -... -... --- / -. . / -. --- / .-. --- -.. ..... --- ... "Ter-
ror" equals "monitor" equals: "All our sense impressions may be
layered over the 26 or so seconds an average human urination
requires." --. ..- -. ..- ..- -.. ..- --.. / --- -... - .-- / -. --- -... -... -.... ..- .-.. --- -..
/ - -..- --. --. -.- / --- -. --- ... .-. -.- --- -.. / ..- -- --- -... -.. --. --- / -. --- ..- .-..
-. ..- / -.-. ..- -.. .-. --- -.. / -- --- . --- .... --.. / ... --- -... -. . --- -.... ..- An
inextinguishable longing and the wind carries her song. - . --. /

-.-. ..- .-.-. ..- -..- . .-.. / -- ..- .- / - ..- -.. / .-.. .-. -... .-. .-. ..- .- .-. .-.. ..- / .... .-.. .
--- -.. / --- ..-. / - ..- -.. / .-... . / - ..- .-.. / --- .--- .--- ..- -.-. ... . -.- / .-. .--- / -
..- .-.. Few have known community, but instead we have politics,
shadow of technologies dedicated to manufacturing nonenti-
ties. ..-. --- -... / - ..- .-.. / .... -.- --- ... / . / --- ..-. .-.. .-. ..- -.. .-.-. / --- --. /
-.. --- --. ..- .-.. / ..-. -... --- / .... --- .-. .-. ..- .-.. .-.-. / *Music of hoboys*
is under the stage. --- ... .-.. - / .-. -... --- ..- .-. .-.-. / --- .-.. / .-.- ..- --.
/ .-. -... --- ..- ..- ..- -.. / ..- -.. / .-. ... --- -... -. ..- - / --- --. / -- ..- - / -.
--- -- .-.-. / *[Digging.]* -. ... . / .... -. --- .-. .-. ... ..- -.-. / -. --- -.. ....
/ .... --- -.. / - ..- -.. / -. --- ... .- .-. ..- -.. / -. --- -- / .... ..- ... .- -.-. /
--- .-.. / - ..- -.. / . -.- .-.- ..- / ..- ..-. .-.. .-. ..- -... ... --- ..- .... / -. -.. .- ..- .-..
/ ..- ... ..- ..- -.. / -.-. --- .-. ..- -. .-. ..- .... / . / --- -... .-. -. ..- .-. - ..- -... Every
being's two faced: One's turned out, one in. -.. --- -.- --- -.- --- -.-. .
--. -. --- -.. . .-.. --. / -- --. --- / --- -.. .-. --- .... .-. -- --- -.. / -. --- -.- --- --- -..
/ -.- --- -. -. -. -. -. . .-. --- -.. / -- --- --- -- -- ..- .-.. --- -.- .-.- / . .-.- --- /
--- -. -.- / -.. --- --- -. -. --- -.- --- ... -. ..- -. -. -. ..- .-. / -.. --- / . -.. . -. --- --.
. .... / .... --- / .... --- / -- --- ... --- -.- --- / .-. --- --- -... ..- / .... --- /
.-- --- ... --- To starboard I padlocked on a tiny splinter edged
with white—a cockleshell like the one we are in designed and
fabricated and riveted together to carry souls away from where
they belong into majuberous elements where they've no kin.

The big commotion was getting pretty close. -.- --- -. . .-.. /
.... --- / .-. .--- -- -. . .-. ..- -. -.. / -.. -. --. / -.- .-. --- -.. ... . --- .-.-. / *Alarums.*
[They fight. E— *falls.]* --- .-. .. / . .... --- -.. ..- --. / -- --- -.- -. --. . -.. ... -.. ..
/ -.. --- / -- --- -.- --. . . .-. .. -.. / .... --- -.. -. . . / .... --- / --- .-. ..- / - --- .-.
--- .-. .. / -.. --- / .-.. . .-.. .-. --- -. -. --- ... -. . --- .. .-. -. -. .-. --- -... .-. -. ../ .-
--- ... --- For a long time this had been this happy honky hunting
ground. - -.. -... -. --- -.. / ... --- / .-. --- .-. ..- .-. .-. -.. .- ... ../ -- --- .-.. /
..- / -- --- --. ..- .-. .-. ..- / .-. -. --. ..- -.. .-. .-. / - ..- / .-. ..- .-. ..- -... ../ -- -.. -... -.
.-.. / . .-.. .... .-.. .-. --- -. ..- .-. --- -.. ..- -- ..- -.. ..- .-. .-.-. / *[M—]* *is shut in.*
.--- ..- / ... --- . / .-. ..- -.. .- ..- / -- --- -.- ..- -. ..- . ..- / ..-. . . / ..- . --- .
.... / .... -.- -.. / -. -.- ..- --- -.- ..- ..- .-. --- -.. ..- / .-. -. .... -.- -.. / .-. --- -.-
..- -.. .. -.. .... / -- --- -.- -- ..- -. .-. / .-. ..- - ..- / ..- ..- .. -.. ... ..- Though its
application is scaled, power is key to sustained deceit. To lose it

in a superficial lie simply halts its immediate utility. We are still "on the ground" and can step back and introduce an alternate subterfuge to divert attention from the bent area.

Of course there isn't any fixity equivalent to land in the realm of cons; rather all's swimming. That means that while we stay afloat we may count on a certain residual surface turbitude to keep the dupe rattled, ripe, ITDAFOS. Certainly when a full-blown viral con's going its manufacturers may count on such turbo momentum.

However a real loss of power, such as a change in governance or systemic change in information technology, may cause over time a substantial drain. This may tear the MK(s) away. If the game's not swiftly adapted, a gap may form and its roots exposed.

For the dupe it'll be the equivalent of that fairy-tale moment: "The scales fell from her eyes." Such moments of clear vision may become attached retrospectively to the residual power of the former deluded state, which may result in violent reversal.

But this is rare. Again, one may count on momentum as well as the near universal human tendency to prefer anything, including delusion, to facing the potential emptiness its evisceration may leave.

To use that momentum, however—assuming we do not actually want an outright collapse and disruption of life pattern and other "inconveniences" (inc. criminal prosecution)—we must control the terms of its dismemberment. Information surges must be applied, degrading the signal by methodically introducing ample ambiguities: or cast adrift so many mildly plausible lines to follow that substance becomes intermingled interminably with shadow. Or if we control the images we control the culture. Moreover we may even cut the lie open ourselves, which serves the function of both separating us from its wreckage as well as seeming to be the hero of the story: Or the frog becomes a prince.

History is rife with such master reverse cons, just as it is with revolutions, statecraft's crash sites.

TLAR. .-. -.... ..- --- / --.- -..- ..- / .... --- -.-. / .-.. -. --- -... --- -... .-.-.- / --- / --.- -..- ..- / .... ..- . / .-. -.... ..- -... .-.-.- / *Draw the Conspirators, and kills M—, who falls; A— stands over him.* ..- --- / --.- -..- ..- / .-. -.-. --- - --- / -.... .-.. .... --- ... ...- ..- -... / .-. -.-- --- --- / .-.-. ..- -.. .... --- -.... / --- / -- --- --- -- ..- -.. .-.. .-.. --- / - ..- / --- -- . --. ---/ --.- -..- ..- / ..- -..- / ...- --- -..- .-.-.- / [*They sit.*] --- / --.- -..- ..- / ..-. --- ... --- -..- .-.-.- / .--. --- - ..- / ....- -... / .-.. --- -... / .-.-. --- -... / .-. --- .... -..- --- ... . - --- - ..- / ..- .... .-.. ..- / .-.. . -... --- -.. .--- Welcome to earth house. Welcome to hive of tragic activity. -. --- .--- ..- / --- -- ..- -... . .-. --- -.. --- / .-..- --- -... -.... --- -..- ....- / --- / .--. -.-. ..- .... --- - ..- ... --- I am a stainless fish in the fountain a pure virgin gasped.

Stillness. Silence.

Pink light through closed eyelids. --. ..- --. ..- -.-. ..- -.. / .-- ..- -... - ..- -.. / -.-. ..- . -..- / -- ..- -. -... / --- - ..- -... / .-- ..- -.. -.. / .-- ..- -... ..-. .-- ..- -... / -. --- -.-. ..- -.. / . -. -- / - ..- / ..- -- -. -.-. --- -.... ..-. -.. -.. ..- -.- .-.-.- / (*Reads.*) . -..- -.. / -.- ..- . -.. ..- -... / -- .-.. / .-. .-- / --.. -.- / - ..- ..- -.. -.. / ..... --- -.. .- -.. -.... -.. / --. ..- --. -.-. .-. -.- .-.. .-.- -.. / - . -.. --. .- -.- Consciousness is oracular and built underground in the beehive style derived from African ghosthouses. Dressed in rose petals psychomantic priestesses preside in this navel shrine through which the spiraled python's cunningly entwined.

A lapping sound is heard in the dark. Queer, bat-like voices. The peeping and muttering of souls. -- --- -.. .-. -... ..- / ..-. . --.. . / --- -.- .-.-.- / ..... . / --- -..- / ....- / .-.. --- -.- .-.- ..- / --- -.- / -.- --- -.. / .-- --- -.. / --- -.. -... .--- ..- .-.. .-.- -.-. --- --- / ..-. ..- / -- / -.- --- / --.. --- -.. / ---.. / .-.. --- -. . / -.- --- / -.. --- -... / -- --- -.. - -.-- --- / --- -.. .- ..-. -.-. / --- -. .-- .-.. .-.- -.. / -.- .-.. . --- --- -..- -.. / .-- .-- --- / --- --.. .-.- / ..- .-.. -.- --- -.- -.- --- -... .-.-.- / *Low march within.* -- .-- ..- -... / .-. --- / -.- --- / --. -. -.- .--- ..- / --- / -.. .-.- ..- -.. / -- . .--- -.- -..- ..-. .-. / -.- . / --. ..- -..
A startling thought occurs to me: Maybe they don't know much more about us than we do about them.

Perhaps the thoroughly developed policy of no one knowing

anything he or she doesn't absolutely have to know is a two-way street—even to the point where they aren't entirely sure who they are themselves.

We all slide. Like beef. Slabs. Slip and float. Off. -. .-... ..- -.- /
-.-. ..- .... --.. ..- ... -.. ..- -.- / --- .-.. ... My kingdom for a coke. .... . -.
--- .-... ... --- -. / - . / -- --- -.. --- / -.-. ..- -... . . -... . / -..-- --- -.. --. / .-..
..- -... .-. -.-. .-.. -.-. -.- / -.-. ..- .-.. --- ... --- / .-.. ..- -... --- -- .-.. --- ....
/ .-... ..- -... .... ..- -.-. -.-. .-.. .-.-. / .-- --- -.-. .-.. -.-. / -.-.- --- -.. --. / .-.
..- -.-. --- .... .-.-. / P— *stabs him.* --- -.- -..- / -- ..- ... . .-. --- .-.. / ..- -..
--. -.- --- -.- / - . -.- ..- .-. -.- -.-. -... --. / .-- ..- -.. -. -.-. --- -.. / -- -.-. .-.. . --- -...
--- / - --- -... / -.- ..- -... --- .-- --- .-.- / -- -.- / .-.. -.-.- / -.-. ..- -... -.-.
. .-. --- -... --- / ..... . --- .-. --- / ..... --- ... --- -- / ..... --- -.- --- / - --- ...
--- -- / .-.-. . -.-. . -... --- -.. / - ..- -... ..- -.- --- Only the money's real.
To watch the money dance. To dart as fast as money. As light.

To ride, without wetting our knickers, the hand that stabs into every wallet.

But its life cannot be seen. It's really zero and moonbeams.

But the money alone is real to which flesh appends and on which the beast feeds.

"Be still!" ... -..- --- -. --. . --- .-.-. / *[Whispering.]* .-.-. ./ ..- / --.-..- .
.-.-. / -. --- / .-.. --- -... ... --- -... ..- .-.-. / *[Knocks.]* -.. ..- .... -..- -..
--- / -.... ..... .-. .--- .... .-. --- .-.-. / .-. -.-. / .-. --- .... --- / ..- / -.-.- -.. ..-
.... .-. --- .-.-. / .-. ..- -.. -. . -.. -. -.-. .-. --- -.. / ..- / -- --- -.. ... .-. --- / .-.-.
..- / -. --- / - .... .-. .. ..- .... --- / . ... / ..... -.. --- / .-. ..- -.. -.. .-. --- / -.-.
..- -..- ..- .... ..- -.. ..- . .-.-. / *Low alarums.* --- ... .-. .-.- -.. ..- / -.-. ..- ....
.-.. . ..- / --- ... .- ..- --- .-. ..- / --.- -.- .- ..- .... .-. --- / .-. .-.- It was a
closed body van, a wooden bench attached to each sidewall. He said not to talk or make any noise, slammed the hatch and we farted off. Sounds of heavy street traffic and constant stopping and starting. Then long stretches of donkey-foxtrot dittybopper hours watching brain cells enter a RDF. A smoke crack. The beinhaus. -- ..- -.. -.- .- --- . / --- - --- ... --- -. / ....- .-. ..- -... .-. . / -..
--- -- --- / ..... . --- .-. ..- --- / .-. -.-. ..- -.. -.-. ... --- -.. -.. .-. --- -.. / --- -.- --- -..
/ -- --- -.. -.. ..- .-. --- .-. . / - ..- -.. -.-. ..- -.- -.. / -.-.- -.-.- .-. .-. -.- -.- --- -.. .-.-. / -.-.- ....

--- -.. . .-. / ..... .--- .-=-. .--- / - .-- -- . .-- . .--- -.. / .-.. .. .--. .-=. .- .-- ....

.-.-.- / [*Runs on his sword.*] --- -... --- -... --. / . .-.. -.- / -- -... .... . .--- /

.-.. .--- .-=. . / .- .-.. -.. .-. --. --- -.. / .--.- .... .--- -. . / .-.. .. -... --- .-.- -. . .-.. /

. .--- / -- .- .-. -.. .-=- .- .-. --- / -.- .- .... -. -- --- -.. .-.-. / -. .--- -.. .-. .-.- -..

/ -.. .. -.. --. .--- -.. .--- -.. .-- .-. --- .-.-. / . .--- -.. / -. .--- -- --- -.. .-.-. --- / .-.

.- .-.. .--- .-=. / -.- -.. .-.. .-.. .-. -.- / -.- .... . .--- / ..... .- .-. -.. .- -.. .-.. .-- -.-.

--- / - . .-. -.. .-.. .-.. . . .-.-. / -.-. .- .. .--- -.- -.. .-. --- / .-. .--- - --- --. -.- -.- / --- -..

--- -.- The determination to keep the SOP alive sprang in part
from the embarrassment of calling it off. Hiding the mess now
would be like trying to cover a plate of Jell-O with one hand.
We'd need a very big hand or cluster Foxtrot of fisters.

FIDO. --- -. ....- -.-. / .-.. -. .--- -... / -.. . .--- --- / --- -.. .--- -... .- ...-
--- .... / --. -. .--- ... / .-.. -.. . .- ..- -- / .-.. --- .-.- .-.. . ... / --. -.-. .--- -. .--- /
.-.. -... . - / .-.. .. .-. .-. --- -.- --- .... / .-- -... --- -.. --. .... .-.-. / [*Within.*]
-.-. . .-.. ..- / .--- .-.. .-=. .- ..- .... --- -.- / --. -. --- .... .-. .-.-. / -. .-.- .--- --- /
.-. --- -... .- ..... / -- -. .- ..- / --. -. .--- .... / .-- .. .-.- .-.. .-.. --. / .--.. ..- --.
-. ..- .-. .-.- / [*He dies.*] -.-. --- -.-. / .-.. -. .--- -.- / ..... .-.- ..- --- --. .-.- /
.-. --- -... .... / -. .- .... . .-.. ..- .... / .--- .... ..- / ....- / .--. .
-- ..- . / -- ..- --. --. -. -.- / --- --. .-.. --- -.-. / -- . .. . / .--. . .... .- --- / -.-
--- --. -.-. -.- -.. . / .-.. --- --. .-. -. .- --- / -.. .--- --. -.- -.-. .... . The go/
no-go OSM was made long before we left the penthouse. -- ..- -..
/ - .- .-. / .... --- .-. / -- --- -.. --. .- / ..... .-. .- ..- . .-. .- .- -.. / . -.- -. ..- / .
/ .... -.- --- ..- -. .. ..- / ..... . -.- . .- The truth is not omitted: It's where
the absence is, where we are—vents that let the beast breathe.
And we're inside—not extraneous. Centripetal, not fugal, the
suck. -.- --- .-- - --- -.. .- -. / .... --- / .-. -. --- -... --- -.. .- -. .- -.. .-. --
.-.. .-.- -.-. .-. --. .-. .-.. / .-. / -. .-- ..... .-. . ..- .-- It complexes quickly, goes
BVR. It completely sucks. There can be no visualization of the
brain's interior, the many faces moments mount scrambling for
the cockholster, WTFO.

Her head thrown back. --- / .-. --- -- . .-.. -. -. .--- / -.--- / -.-. --- ...
--- / .-. -. --- - ..- / ....- -... / - ..- .-.- .-. --. .. .-- / --- / .-. -. --- -.. .-.. . -...
/ - --- / .-. --- -.. -. .-. -.. .-- .... --- --- / -... --- -.- ..- --- In the end I found
the house and groped cold nosed in the goo up the second-floor

stairs and locked at the end of all the unlighted hallways of the world on a slit of light under a door. The place smelt of boiled cabbage, and I stood there holding my balls, beaded up, BO-HICA. ...- --- / -- -.. ... .-.. -.. -- . -- / - . .-.. / -.. --- -.. / .-. .. .. - -.. .-.. -...
-.. - / --- .-- -.. -.. .-.. .-. .-.. --- -... / .-. -.. .- / --. --- --. --- -... . .-.. --- / -- . .-. .-. --- /
-.. --- --- .... .-.. -... --- Every part of speech is a black hole sucking a hearty psych-op cocktail. .-. -- --- --.- -.. -. .. / ... --- / ... .- . --- / - .. / -.. .-.. .- .... .-.. -... --- / - . ... -... .-. .-. / [Raising his voice.] .... /
-.. --- / .- -. -... .- -.. -... --- / -- . .... --- -... .- --- / --.- -.. -.. .- / -.. --- ... / --- ... .-.
.. .-. .-. . .- --- / -- -.-. .... / . - . / -... .- . -.. . -- . .- -.. -.. .-. .-. --- / - ... / -..
-.. .- .. ..-. - .-. --- / -.. -.-. --- --. .-. --- / --- --. --. . . .-. .-. --- - --- / -.. . --- / -- -.. /
--. -.. .- .... .-. --- -.. --- / -.- . .-. --- / --. --- . .-. --- / - .. / .... --- -.. -.. .-. - ...
.. / -- --- -.. -.. .-.- / .-. . .- .-. .-. -. --- .-. / -- .- .-. - .- -... / --. --- .... .-.
--- - --- / -- --- .... / ... .- -.. / .... / - .. .-. - .- -.. .... --- .-. .-. / .-. .- ... -...
--- / - . --. -.. .-. --- / -.- .-.- Enter the Messenger as before. --- -.. .-
-... .... / .- .. .. --- / .- .... / -..- -.. / .-. .. .- -- --- / - .. / -. --- -.. .-. --- -...
/ -. -- / -.. .- -.. --- -.. --- --.-. -... .- / -. -.- -.. / .- .. ..-. .. -- -.- .. ... --- / --- /
--- .... / - .. . .-. .-. -. --- .... / ... --- -- ... . -.. .- .- .. / -. / -- --- --. -. -.. .- --- -..
. .- --- But how far can I go without telling the truth? How long dangle leads and starts, WAGs, snarls, sparks, farts, fragments of names, whispers of how it really went down—and is still?

The horror to know slow or quick we are coming unhinged—the connections, always at best tenuous, slipping, NMC.

To turn the old key... a tremor. A tremor.

But I only nibble the edge of darkness, sprinkle its crumbs into my pipe bowl and then touching fire suck up where I cannot see just past my nose what remains of this creep show. Train eyes past these words to where in afterburn they singe dystopic, myopic gangrene prismatic capitalist propaganda UYA machine.

POBCAK. .-- --- .-.. -.. - / .- --- .-. .-. --- .- -.. -.. .- .. .- --- / -.- -.
--- -.- . .- -- .-. / .- --- .-. -.. --- .-.. / -.-. --- . .- . --- / -.-. .- -.. .-. .-. / -. .-.. -.-
--- Few things matter. The axes we grind POC. Access to excess. If even only its mouth. .-.. --- / . - --- -. / .. .-. -.. / -. -.. .- .... .-. .... - ..- /

--- .-. -. / -- . -.. --- / ....- --- ... / .. ....- - .... / --- -- / ....- . - / --. ..- -.. --- --
..-. --- -... --- -.. . .-. .-.. / --- ...- / -- . .-.. / ...- . .... .-.- --- -.-.- / [*Raises
her.*] -- . -.. / ...- . .... .-.- --- / -.-. .-. .-. .-.. --- -.. - --- .... / --- ...- / -- . -..
--- / --- -- -. --- -.. / --- .-.-. -. / --- -... --- -.. .-.-. / .-.. ...- --- / -. --- -.. . ....
--- .... / .-. . .... --- .-.. .-. .-... / -- .- ... . --- -.. / ..-. --- -... .... . --. --- / ....
.-.. -.. --- --- -.. - .- .-.. / .-. --- --- -- .-. .-.. / --- .-. -. / - --- -- .-.-. / -. .-.- -..
/ -. - --- -.. / .--- --- --. / -.- -.. -.- - ... . .-- --- / --- ... -.. .- -.. / -- . .-.. / ... .
... .--- --- / --- ... -.. .... - --- -- .-. / ... -- --- - / - / - .- -.. .-.. / ... --- --- .. -.. / .. .-. -..
-..- / --- .-.. .-.. / .-- --- --. . / ... - --- - ... - .. -.-.- / *Drums and trumpets
sound, with great shouts of the people.* - .. .-.. / .-.- --- -.. / . -.. .-.. .-.. ..- /
.... -.-- --- .-.. .-.. .- ..- .-.. ... -.-- -.-. .-.. / .-. --- / -... -.- --- --. -- --- / .-.- . ...
-.-. --- -.- --- / ..-. -... --- --- -.. / - .- .-. -..- .-. ... --- / --- .-. .-. / --- .-. .-. ... / .... .-..
--- / .. .-.- --- .... .-. / -- .- - - / --- -... ... --- .-.-. / [*Enter* G— [*led by*] *an*
Old Man. ....- . / ...- --- .-. -... - .- .-. ... / . .- ... .- -... .- / .-.. . ...-. --- /
.... . - .- .- .-. .- -.- --- --. -.. .- .-. -... -.. --- / .-. .-. --- / -. . --- ..- .- ... --- -.. .- -.. / -..
--- -... / ...- . / -. . --- -... / .... -- -.- .-. .-.. ..... . --. --- / - .. -- -- Cut to scene
of meeting, sounds of nature (monstrous), language, lantern.
Power "naked."

Versus the pattern in which it's become fixed.

Paranoia runs deep through the Salvo. The wreck etched in
mindaches, misfires, zone outs.

Profiles in storage in black boxes. Racks of body parts.

Nobody can see in... in the stillness maggots work.

We can't get dark enough to slip past. Grip what do does.

And sure the waves close, but before they close they wave.
Between thighs marvelous with dew. ..-. --- -.-. ... --- -.. / --- / ---
-... --- - --- / --- -- --- / -.- --- ... --- .-. / .-. --- -... --- / .-. .-.- .--. --- ...
--- -... .- .-.-. / *Sound. Flourish.* --- -.. .. .- ..- / -.-. -.- .... - .-.- -. / -- .
--. -. .-.. / - -.. ..- .... -.- -.. .- -- -.- / .... --- -.. They weren't going to let
him leave. -- --- .- -. / .-. --- -... --- -.. --- -.-. -.- / .-.- / --. ..- .- .-.- -..
/ --- -... / .-- --- .-. -. .- / --- .-. / .-.-. / -.. .-. / ..-. --- -... .- .- -. --- -.. - / .- .- . -.. /
--. .-. --- .-.. .-. .... .- .- . --- -... .-.- .-.. / .-. --- .- . / . ..- . / --. ....- ... . / . ...
--- .-. -.. / --- -... / .- . / .- -... .- .-. --- --- -. .-... .- .-. .-. - / --- .- .-. .- .- -... ---
--. / .-.. .- .-.. ... --- .... .-. - .... / .-.-. -.. / .-.. .-. .-.- --- .- .-. .-. -.-.- /

--- .-. / -.-- -.. / ..- . / -.-. --- -.-. .-- ... ... / -.-- -.. / --. --- -... .-- .-- - - / --. .-- --- .-.. .-- --- -... / . -.. / - -.-. ... -.-. -.. .--- - --- -.-. -.. . .-- -. . / -. .-. . -... --. / -. .-. .-.. .-.. / . .- --. / --. .-.. --- -.- - --- -- --. / [Looking on the jewel.] --- -... / .-- .-- ... -.-- / - - . --- --. / -.-- / - .-.-- - - / ... . .-- ... .. .-- ... --- -.. --. / --. .-- .-- .-- . --- -.. -.. / .--- .- ... .-. .- .... / .-- .-- .-- .-- .-.-- / --- / --. .-.-- - --- / --. .-- .- ... . .-. .-.-.. .-- .-- - -.-. / .-. .-. .-- .-- .-- .-- .-- -... / .-. -. . - .- -.-.. / .-.-- .-. -. / .... --- -.-. .- .-- -.. .-- -.. / .. .-- .-- -.-- / --. --- ... ... --- / --- -.-. / [Dies. F— escapes.] -.... -. .-.. .-- --- -.-. -.... - --- - / - . -.... .-.. .-.. / .-- -.-- --- .- .- . -. / .- ... .- --- -.. / .--. .-- --- .-.-- / -.. .-- --- .-. .- .- .. / -. .- .- -... / .--. / - -.-. / .-.-.- . --- - / -.-- / .. -.. .-.-. --- - / .-- .-- .-.-- . .- / --- -.-. / --- .-. / .- ... .-- / -.-- / --- --- .-- / ... . / ..... .- .-.. -... .-- ... .- .-.. .- ... / .-.- .-.- .- --- -... -.. --- ... .- .-.
We're still in a great place, though at the back of it manacled and hooded—or we're not all cross-dressing, night-goggled psychopaths building a chest of breasts like the medals generals mint and sport at fashion shows. --.. -.-.- --. .. .- --. .. .- --. .. -.. / .-.. ... --- -..
.- .-.. --- -.- / .- .-.. --- / --. .-. .-. .-.. .-.. --- --- -.- / .- .- -.. .-.. -. ... -.. / -.-.
--- -.. .- -.. / --- --. .- . -.. -.. .- .- .-- / .-. ... .- --. .-. --- ... --- -.-- -.-- / -- .- --..
-.. / --- ... - .- -.. / . .- .- .. / ..... -.- -.. .- / .- -.. . .- -.-- -.- .- -.- .- --..
.- .- .-- / --- -.. .- -. --- .- / .-- .-. .-.. --- / .-.. .- -.-. -.. -.- --- -.-. .-. .-.-. / -.-. .- .
-.. .- --- / -.. .-. --- -. .- --- .... -.-. .- .-. --- / --. .- --- . . .-. --. -.. / .-- .-.- .- /
.-. .. .... --- -.. .- .-. .- --- --. -.. / --- -.. .. --- -. .- -.. / --- -. .. . .-. -.. .- -.. / --- --- --.
/ - --- / --.. .- .-. / . -.-. .- -.. .- .- -. / .- -. .- --- -.-- --- / .- .- .-.. .-. --- / --..- .. -... /
.-. --- .-. .- -.-. .- .-.. -.. .- .- .. .-.- / --.. .- - -... / -- --- .- .. .- .. .-.- / --... .- -... /
. .-. .- .... --- .... --- --- .-. --- --. .. .. .- -.. / -.... --- --. .- .- . .-.-.- / [To the Fool.] ...
-.. -.-. -... / - --- -... .-.. - --- -... .-. --- .-.-.- / -. .-- --- . -.-. .- .-.. -.-. / .- -.-.. .- / -. .-.-- .
-.... -... --- -.. .- --- -... .- -.-.-. / . -.-. -... . . -. .- -.-- / --- -. .- .- --- --- -.-. --- .- .- /
.-.-.. --- -- . --. .- -.-.- . --- --. --- -... --.. / - .-. -.-. .- ... . -.-. . .- - -.. --- .-. .- / .- -.-. .-
--- / .-. .- -... --- --- -.. .-. / -... --- .-- .- -... - / .- -... .-.. .- .- .-. -.. .- .- -.-. .- .-. /
-.-. . --- . -... -.. --- --- / .- -.- .-. .- --- / . . .. --- --- -... .- .-. --- -.. -.. ... -. . --- /
.. --- --.. ... .-. .- --. .-. -.. .- .- / . -... .- .- .- .-. .- -... --- .- .-. -.. .-. / --- - -... .-. .... --- .- . --. --- --- .- .-. .- / -... -... . .- .-. / .-- .-- --- .-.- .- -.-. --- .-. .-. /
/ --.. . --- / -.-.- .- --- -... .- .-. / .. .-. -.-. .-- .- .-- .-.- .. .-. .- -... .- / --- .-- --- .-. / -... -... . --- -.. /
--- --- -. .-. --- .-. .- .-.- .- -. -... .- .- -.... / -... -.. -.-- .- .- .-. / --.- -... .- -. -... / --.. .-.- .- - /
. .-.. --- .... --- --- .... .. -... --- .- .- -.. / -.... --- --- .- . -.-. .-. .- -... --.. .- .-.-. / [To the Fool.] ...
--- -.- -... / - --- -... .-. .- - --- -... .-. --- -.-.-. / -. .-. --- -... . -.-.-. / .-- .- -.... -.- .-- / -- -.-.. .
-.... -.-. .-- --- -... .- . -... .- .- .-.- .-. --. -... .- .-. .- .. --- --- -... / .- --. . -... .-. --- .. -.-. / . .-. --.
-.-.-. . -.. . / --- -... .- . .- - / -.... .- .-. .. . .. -.-. / .- -. .-- -.-- .- . .- --- / -.- .- .- . /
--- / -.- -.-. -... --- .. -.-. .- -... / -.-.. -.-. .- --- / .- --- -.-.. --- --. .. -.-.-- . .-. -.-. .-.-- -. .- .-.-.- /
-.-.- -. --- .-. .-.. .- --- --... -.- -... .. --- -.-.-. / .- - .-. --- .-. .- -... / --- --. -. .-.-. ..... --- --- -.-. .- .... /
.. - --. -... .- -... --- -.. -. -... -... .-.- / .- -.. .- .-.. - -. --- -.. -.. . .- -- -- .- / --- --. -... .-.-. .- .-.. --. . -... /
/ --. --- . / -.-. .- -- .-. -... .- .-.- / .- -.. .. -... -.-. .. .-. -... .- -.... .-- .- / --- --- -. .-- .-.. -.-.- --. .- .-. --- -.-.-.-. .
--- -.-.- The unslit frame X.
We don't want the children to see this.

What grownups will do to goose the tomtom. -- --- -.. --. .... ..- -
..- / ..- -.. / -- ..- .... .-.. ..- -... / -- ..- -.. / ..-. --- -... / - ....- / .-.. . ...
..-. --- ... - ..- .-.-.- / [*Keeping some gold.*] .... .-. ..- .-. . --- .... . .-.. ..- .-.
/ -... ..- --. ..- .... / ..- -.. / .-.. .... ..- ..- ..- -.. / ..-. --- -... .... --- -- .-. .-.-.- /
--- --. / ....- / -. ..- --- -... - --- -.. / -- --- -.. --. ..- / --- -- ..- -... . .-. --- ...
-.. / .-.. .. ..- .... .-. ..- ..- / ..... .-. ..- --- -.. / -. --- ... ..- ... --- .-. / .-. .. --- / - ..- --- -.. -..
..- / --- ... -- . ..- .. ..- .... . -.- .-. / ..... --- / -- --- -.. -.. ..- / -. .-. .-. ... ..- / ..-.
-.. --- -.. --- .-. .-. . --- -.. .. ..- -... .-.-.- / *Drum, trumpets* [*sound*] *flourish.*
A piece goes off [*within*]. -.. --- -... / --- .-. . / - ..- -.. / -- ... ..- -.. ..- -...
..- ... ..- ..- / . .-. -.- ..- / ..- -... / ..... --- -- / -.-. . ...-. ... --- - ..- / .-. ..- .... / -.
.... ..- -- / ..-. --- -... ... --- --. ..- -... .... / ..... -.- --- ... / --- ... ... / -... ..- .-.
--- -... --- .-. ... . --- -.. ..... .-. .-. / -. ..- --- --- / -. ... --- -... -.. -... . .-.. -. / ..-. --- -...
...- ..- -.. -.. ..- .... The gamblers all get rich, the workers poor.

That guy in the white t-shirt, he looks like a working man.
Not too muscled—slight build but wiry—a bit roughed over,
like he's seen hard times. That street-camp bruised look—a real
cugine—the whole "on the waterfront" mystique. Tough men
hauling fruit off the boats. -.- --- ... . -.. / ... . -.. -.. --- / .---
--- / -. --- -.- -.- --- .... / ..-. . -... -- --- / ..... .-. .--- -... - . -... --- . .-.
--- - The wash—white noise—overinformation—to bury it in
media. Hard anymore to grasp. Has gone over the falls. Except
stay where it appears, on the lip. To loose our jaws. Our brains.
Eye sockets.

Lose the door and its jams or whatever. Pry the wad out. The
interval. Come up raw with the head of the mushroom.

0"-0'-0"-0'. .---- ----. ----. .-.-.- / .... --- / .... --- .-- --- -.-.- / -.. --. /
.-. .--- --- --. .-. --- .-. --- .-. ..- --- --- -.. / .... ..- ..- .... / .... --- / .-. ..- -.- --- ... .-. --- -.. /
-.. --- / -.- --- .-. ..- .-.. .-. --- ..- --- -.. / -.. ..- --. / -- --. --- / .-. ..- --- --- --- .-.-.- /
--- -.. --. / - --- -... --- .-.. / .-. ..- --- --- ... . .--. ..- --. / -- --- -.. .-. . ..... / . ....
--- -.. ..- --. / -- --- --- -.. -.-. --- .-. ... --- -.. / -- -.- ..- --- -.- -.. --- -. . . -.. ..- / --- ...
--- -.. -.. --- ...- / -.-. --- -.. ..- -.. .-. --- / -- --- -.. -.. --- --- .... / .-. --- -.- --- -.- -.. -..-
--- -.. .-./ .... . .-.-.. --- / ..... --- / -.- --- -.. ..- / .-.-.. --- -... ..- -.. / .-. ..- --- .... .-.-. ..- .-..
.-. ..- / - . .-. .-. . . .-. / --- -... -.. / .-. ..- --- --- .-. --. --- --- .-. --- / -... ..- -... / .-. --- --- -..
. .... --- -... -... / .-. --- --- -... .-.. / .... --- / --- -... -.. --- / -... ..- -... / -.. ..- --- .-.

... ..- -.... / -.-. -.- ... -.- .-.-.- / *Alarum afar off, as at a sea fight.* -.. --.
-..- -.. . .-.. / -. .--- -.- --- .-. -.. / --- -.. --. / .--. --- -.- ... / -.-. .- .-.. -. .- ...
/ .... --- ... -.-. --- -. ... -.. --. / .-.. --- --- / -- . -.. .... --- -.. / .--. --- --. --- ...
. .-.. . -.. / --- -.. --. / -.-. --- -.. --- .-.- --- - / --- ... . --- .-. / --- .-.. /
--- -.. --- -.. / -.. --- -.... . .-.. --- / --- -.. --. / -- --- ... --- .-. --- .... / -.. --- /
-.. . .-.. .- - / -.-. --- -.... -. / .... --- / .-. --- -- --- -- --. . . .- .. --- -.. /
-.. -. / .... . .-. . .--- / .-. -.- -.-. -.. .- --- -. / -.. . .- --- --- .-.- / -.- .- --- -.- -.. - .
-.. -. / .... --- / .-. --. --- --. . . .-. --- -.. / -.. -. / - --- .... --- .-. --- -.. --. /
.- ... .- -- .- -.. .-.. -.. --- / -.- --- .... --- -.-.- .-. --- .... .- --- / .-. -.- --- ... --- - /
-.. . --. / .... --- / -.- --- .-. -.-. --- .-. --- --- / -.. --. / .--- ..- -.. -.. .-.- . . .... But
it's not just bread but energy of which food's a form, as we are
ourselves the energy inextricably interwove with the affairs of
the universe governments perform.

Yet we give it up, replaced by a fiction called "The People,"
mask of corporate bureaucracies to which we cough up our
souls. . ...- --- -.- .... / .-.. -.. --- -.- .- ..- ... .- -.. .. -.-. / -.-. -. / - .- .-. .... /
--- ..- --- -.. .-.. .-.. -.. --- -.. .-.. .. / .- .- / .-. ..- / .-. .-. .- / .-. -. -. --- -.. .- .- ... .. --- .-. ... /
-- --- . .... / ... .. / .- .-. --- -.- .... / .-. -. -. .- -.- .-. -. .- -.-. -. .- -.. / --- / .---- .- .-.
.- -.-. / ... ... -.- --. .-.. / -- --- . . / .-. .- ..- ... .- .... / .-. -. -. .- -.- -.- -.- .-.. / ..- -. /
.... -.-. .- / ...- --- -. ... .- .-.. / .... ..- / .-. .--- --- -.- -.- -.- -.-. ... .- / .-. .- -.. /
...- --- -.. .... / .- ..- ... -.- -... ... ..- / ...- --- -.- ... / .-. .- -... .- / .-.. .. .- -.-. / -
..- / -- ..- .... / --- -.-. .-. ... -.- -. -. ...- .-. . ..- .... / -.-. ..- .- -... .-.-. / *Storm and
tempest.* ..- .-. / -- .- .- .. .- .. .- -. / ... --- .... / ..- -.. .. .... --- -.. .- .. /
--- / .-. .. -.. -. .- -. / .- .. ..- .. .-. -. -.. .. -.- --- -.. / ..- .. .- .. / .--- .- /
... .- --- . .... / .... .- .- / --. .-. --- -.. / .--- / .-. -. .-. --- -.. .-. .-. . .-. / - ..- /
.... . / . .... / -.-. --- / - .- .... / .-. .-. --- -- -- -. .- .. ... .- .... / ..- -.. / .-. -... --- -..
.-. .- / --- .-. -. .-. ..- / .... .-. -.. .-. .- / .-. .- --- -.-. .-. ..- / ... .- ..- / ... .- --- ... ...
-. .. .-.-. / .-. .--- --- .-. .... / ... .- .. / ... .- --- / -.-. -.- --- .-. -.. .. ..- / .-.
-. .-. -.. .-. ... ... / - --- -. .. .-.. / ... ..- / -.. ... - .... She roared her song. She knew
it had no end because neither had her journey form.

Her song had no words, returning thousand-fold echoes
through the sunken ruins of speech and ritual. ..- / .-. .. -.... . ...-..
..- / ..- / ..- / .-.. -.. --- -.-. --- / --- .... / ..-. .. .. --- ..... / -.. --- -.. / ..- / ..- ..- ....
.-.. --- Information's dazzling: a music that calls to a light behind

it, more than any pattern.

Stepping back and back, we're specks now.

In fact, we disappear.

That's the magic. Its act can be caught at any moment it's there not there. Life's magic because of this. It's the center not end—or drop or result.

And there is no beginning either, but I can get us borne into the infinity of the shapes of its flow from whence we know— namely, start—an actuality. .-- --- -... --- -.. / . .-. -. / -- . .-. -. / ..- -... . -.. -.. .- -... .. / ..... . -.. . - / - . .. / -. .-.- .-.- ..- / ..-. .. .- ... --. .. ..- / -.-. -.... . ...- / -..- -.. -.. / --. . -... --- .-. .. ..- -- / -. .-. --- .- -... / -. --- -- -.-. -.-. -... -.... --.

I deny them categorically. Defected. I can't tell everything. Apparently. No ammo. Painted with markings. No record strike. Abandoned. -.- --- .-.. ..- / -- .-. .-. ..- -.. / .-.. ..- / .-. -.-. --- ... ..- / -..- --- -.. / .-. . .. .-. --- / .-. -. -. --- -.. ..... / - ..- .--. .-. -. ... -- / .-. -.-. --- -.-. / - .- .-. -.. / ... --- ....- / --- -.- .-. ..... . - --- -.. / .-. -.. ... -.. / .-. -. -. -. .- ..- / ..-. --- -.-. .-.. -.. / .... --- .-.- -.. ..- / ..... .-. --- -.. .- ..- ..... / -.. .-. --- -.. / ..- .-. -.-. --- ... ... --- .-.-.- / -- .-. . / . -- . . -... --- -.. / -- --- -.. .- ..- .. / .-. --- --- -.. -.-- / .-. -. -. --- -.. / .-. --- --- / ... ..- .--. .-.. -- .- / --- .. / . / -.-.-- / .-- ..- .-.- ..- --- / -. .-. --- -.. -.-- / [Pointing at O—.] -..- --- -.. / .-. --- .-.-. .- .. . / - .- -.. --- -.. / -- / --- -.. .- . / .-. -.-. --- -.-. / -.-. .-.- --- -. -.. .. -.. / -.. --- -.. -.. / ..... .-. ..- .- --- / ..- .-.- -.-. --- -.. / .- .-. - ..- ..- / - -.-- -.-- / Enter Ghost [in his night-gown]. -.- --- -... .- ..- / -.. --- -.. / --- -... .- .-. -... .. -.. .. / ..- --- -.-. .... / .-.- ..- -.-. .. ..- / ..... --- -.. .. / ..... --- -.. ..... / --- -.-. -.-- / -.... --- .-.. --. / -. / -.- --- -.. .-.- ..- .-. -... .. / .- --- -.. .-. -. / .-.-- --- / --- .-. -.- / -.- -.-. . / -- --- -...

"We're all, to some degree or another, brainwashed by the societies we live in, and the mass emotions of any one time—almost impossible to slip—seem the noblest, best and most beautiful," she comments. "Yet within a year they crumple, supplanted by some new war-fed fantasy." ..... . -... .- -.. / ..- .- .. ..- -- / .... --.. .. -- -.-. .. -.. / .- -- --.. .- -.-. -.-. .- --- .-.- ..- .. ..- The occasional loud retort of a backfire washed over the camp.

All the Americans started crying.

We're going in. ..--- ----- ..... .-.-.- / [*Rises and walks aside.*] -..-
--- -- . .-.. / .-- --- --- / -- --- -... . .-.. .. .-.-.- / .-.. .-.- / -.. --- -.. / -. -. --- .
/ .-. -.-. -... --- / - . / -- .. .-.-.- / - .. .-- ..- --- / -.... . -- --- -.. .. .-- -... .. / .
-.. / --.- -.-. .-. .. ..-.. --- / -- --- -.. .- --- / .... --- -... .- --- / .-.. -. .. / . -.. /
.-.. -..- --- / --- .... -.. .-.. --- / -.. --- -.. / ... / -- ... -.. .... . --- / - . /
-..- -.. . / .-.-. --- -... .-. . ...-.-.- / *They heave* A— *aloft to* C—. --- /
...- .. ..- .-. -... .. ..- / .... ..- / -- . ..- / - --- -... -.. .. ..- .-.-.- / *Enter* B— *in his*
orchard. ... --- / .-. --- -... --- -.. --- / - .. ... / . --- -.-. .-. . / .-.. .. .-- -... -...
--- / ..... / ..-. --- -.. . --- -.. . --- .-.-.- / -- .--- / ..... .--. -.. --- -.. ..- I could
see the bright red flush spreading over his neck and up behind
his ears. -.. . .-.. .. ..- / -- -. .-. --- -.. . --- / .-- --- -.- --- Time becomes the
recognizable with which we're most involved, that last element
to be lined, and as a species wait at the brink of that which will
free us.

What birds sing: "is-is-is."

There is no more we can register than this—or do.

Or fake at best, before feeling sick.

There is nothing to transcend. Nothing to transform. There's
no other, no duality in what we form.

Queer, though, how driving away we seemed to have less than
we had driving in. .-. -..- ... --- .... / --- -.. .-.- ..- / .... --- ... / .-.- -... .. ..- ---
-.-.- .-. ..- -.- -... / ..- . .- -- -- .. ..-. .... / .... --- -.. .-. .-.- .-.- . -.. ..- -- / --- .-. . /
-. --- -.-. ..- / .-.- -.-. -.. --- .. .-.. ..- .-.- [*Faints.*] --- --. --- / .-.. -.. .--. --- . .- ..-.
/ --- -- -. .. --- / .... .-. .-. -.. .- -.. ..- -- / .. .-.- / .-.. -.-. / -.. --- -.. / .-.-
.. .-. .. . -- -.- .... / -.- .-. / .-.- .-. -.- .-. -.- -- / ..... .-- -. .... .- . -- .-. -..
.-.. / .-.. --- -- -.-. -.- --- -- / ..... . -.. -- .-. ... . / -- -.. .-. .-. .-.- -.. ..- .-.-.- /
.. .-.. ..- .-. . .... .-.. . / --- -- -.. ..- -- / .-- ..- --- -.. / - --- -.. -.-. .- ... .-.-.- /
-..- -... --.. -.-.. .-. ..- -- / .-. .-. .-.. -.. --- . .-. .. .. .- .-.- / .-. ... . .. / ..- .- --- -.-
. .-. -.-. .... / ..- -.. .- .... .-. -.. ... .-.- / --- -- ..- .-.. / - ..-. .-. ..- / - -. --
-... ... . / .-. .-. -.- -.. / --- .-. -.- --- -... / --- --- .-- --- / .... --- --- ..- --- / ...
--- .-. -... .- .. -- --- -.. -.. -.- -- / --- / ..- -.- .-. ... -.. .. ..- -... . .-. -.- -.. .... / .-. -.- . .
.... / .-. --- -.. -. . -.. ..- --- -.. -.. .-. / --- .... .-. .-. ... --- -.. .-. .-. -.- -.. / -.
--- -.. -.. --- -.- ..- / ... --- -.. -.. . .-. .-. .- .... / .-. --- .-. -.- .- -.- -- .-.-.- / - --- /
-- --- -.. ... ..- -- / .-. .- -.- --- -- / -. .-.- .-. / -.. -... --- -.. - . / .-. --- --- -- ..-

-.. - --- .-.. / ..-. --- . -... -.-- / ..- --. --- / .... ..- -... -- --- -.. . -.-. -..- .... /
.-.. -..- . .... .-.-.- / *She sings.* ...-. --- .-. / -.-. ..- -.. ..- - . .-. --- .-.. / .-.. .
-.-. . / --. -... --- .-... . --- .... .-.-.- / [*A bell rings.*] --- / --- ...- ..- / --- -...
-- . .... / -- ..- . .... / .-. -. --- . .-.. / .-. --- ... ... --- .-.-.- / .-.. -.- / .... --- ...
.-.. -..- / --- .-... --.- -.-. ..- / . -.. / -. --- -.-. . .-.. -.- / --- -... --. -.-. -- ..- -..
.-.. -..- -- / --- -... -- --- / ..- .-. / .-. --- -... / -- ..- -.- -- / . .-. . Well,
let me say then, give a word picture of the emotion we have just
experienced: You act alone.

SAM TRUITT was born in Washington, DC, and raised there and in Tokyo, Japan. He holds degrees from Kenyon College, Brown University and the State University of New York. He is the author of five books of poetry and been the recipient of the 2010 Howard Fellowship, two Fund for Poetry grants and the 2002 Contemporary Poetry Award from the University of Georgia. His works in digital language arts include "transverse," "shaft/state state/shaft," "Days" and "Dick: An Oblique Kennedy Conspiracy Countdown," an audio-visual interpretation of *Dick*. Sam Truitt has worked as a stagehand, audio technician, private investigator, carpenter, teacher and is currently a guest lecturer at Bard College and the Executive Director of Station Hill of Barrytown in the Hudson Valley, where he lives with his wife and daughters. For more, including links to other works: samtruitt.org.

BOOKS FROM LUNAR CHANDELIER PRESS

The Cheapskates by Jerome Sala 2014
Radio at Night by Laurie Price 2013
Tiny Gold Dress by John Godfrey 2012
Earth after Earth by Toni Simon,
with drawings by the author 2012
Deliberate Proof by Vyt Bakaitis 2010
petals, emblems by Lynn Behrendt 2010
Homework by Joe Elliot 2010

CPSIA information can be obtained at www.ICGtesting.com
Printed in the USA
BVOW04s0722180314

347939BV00001BA/5/P